Climbing

Memories of a Missionary's Wife

By
ROSALIND GOFORTH
(MRS. JONATHAN GOFORTH)

Evangel
Publishing House
Nappanee, Indiana 46550

Climbing: Memories of a Missionary's Wife
By Rosalind Goforth

Copyright 1940, 1996, 2008 by Tyndale University College and Seminary. All
rights reserved. First edition 1940. Second edition 1996. Third edition 2008.

Second edition published by Bethel Publishing.

Published by
Evangel Publishing House
2000 Evangel Way
P.O. Box 189
Nappanee, Indiana 46550
Phone: (800) 253-9315
Website: www.evangelpublishing.com

Unless otherwise noted, scripture quotations are from the Holy Bible, King
James Version.

ISBN 978-1-934233-06-1 (previously published by Bethel Publishing,
ISBN 978-0-934998-59-8)

Library of Congress Control Number: 2008941600

13 14 15 16 17 EP 9 8 7 6 5

Introduction

I spent some particularly enjoyable moments recently re-reading Rosalind Goforth's CLIMBING. It stirred happy memories of my own childhood in China. It gave me fresh insights into that intrepid band of missionaries who, braving long separations from home, interminable sea voyages, difficult languages, bandits, and hostility and suspicion on all sides, still *went*. And their fruits do follow them!

I am deeply grateful to Mary Goforth Moynan for promoting this little book as faithfully and tirelessly as she has. We will all be the richer spiritually for it.

My favorite story from this book CLIMBING is when Rosalind suddenly decided she had to rebel and show her husband that she must have her way *sometimes!* She left him in the middle of evangelistic meetings, to go and visit a friend a few hours south by train.

But opening her Bible the next morning to memorize her usual verses, Rosalind was startled to read in Ephesians: "Wives submit yourselves unto your own husbands as unto the Lord." Finding that the next train back to her home in Changte, left in half an hour, she dashed away—and caught it!

On reaching her destination, imagine her surprise to find her husband standing on the platform! "Why Jonathan," she cried, "how did you know I was coming?" He replied with a happy twinkle in his eye, "Oh, I knew you would come!"

This whole story gives a sweet intimate glimpse into the home life of two of God's remarkable servants— Jonathan and Rosalind Goforth.

Coming across another little gem, I copied it. It was a study Mrs. Goforth did on what God does with our sins. Later, when I showed it to my husband, he asked for a copy. "I can use that," he said. And he did.

Ruth Bell Graham

CALL BACK!

If you have gone a little way ahead of me, call back—
'Twill cheer my heart and help my feet along the
stony track;
And if, perchance, Faith's light is dim, because the
oil is low,
Your call will guide my lagging course as wearily
I go.

Call back, and tell me that He went with you into
the storm;
Call back, and say He kept you when the forest's
roots were torn;
That when the heavens thundered and the earth-
quake shook the hill,
He bore you up and held you where the very air
was still.

O friend, call back and tell me, for I cannot see your
face;
They say it glows with triumph, and your feet bound
in the race;
But there are mists between us, and my spirit eyes
are dim,
And I cannot see the glory, though I long for word
of Him.

But if you'll say He heard you when your prayer
was but a cry,
And if you'll say He saw you through the night's
sin-darkened sky—
If you have gone a little way ahead, O friend, call
back—
'Twill cheer my heart and help my feet along the
stony track.

—Selected

CONTENTS

CHAPTER I

A MOTHER'S INFLUENCE

And when by His grace ayont the bricht sun,
The race here is feenished, the vict'ry won,
Not mine be the meed of the Maister's "Weel
  dune,"
    But Mither's.

　　　　　　　　　—Ailsa Craig

THE FIRST PICTURE can scarcely be called a
memory; rather let it be just a family legend.

Rose Cottage, so called from the wealth of
trailing roses enveloping it, was situated (so I
was told) "as near the beautiful Kensington Gardens as could well be." Here, on May 6, 1864
an interesting, if miniature, reception was in
progress.

The center of attraction, a wee mite of human-
ity but a few hours old, was surrounded by her
seven brothers and three sisters. The extreme
ruddiness of the baby's complexion led all quickly
to decide that her name be called "Rosie" (alias
Rosalind). The children were about to file out
as they had entered when one of the older boys
announced solemnly and impressively, *"Now,
children,* WE *must bring this one up right!"*

9

Alas! the immediate years that followed, of almost constant petting on the one hand and merciless teasing on the other, of which the *bringing up right* consisted, developed to an alarming degree a naturally imperious and passionate nature.

But Mother understood! How often when others were clamoring that I should receive a severe chastisement for some grievous misdemeanor, Mother would draw me close to her, and, as I sobbed out for her alone to hear, "O Mother, I do, I do want to be good; I do want to be good," I could feel her arms draw me closer as she whispered: "Some day, Rosie, some day it will all come right."

Then would follow the punishment, but in Mother's way, which was to have me to sit alone in the quiet drawing room while I memorized Bible verses to suit the offense. If it had been an outburst of temper, it would be verses such as:

> He that is slow to anger is better than the mighty; and he that ruleth his spirit, than he that taketh a city.[1]

On one occasion when I had hurt seriously the arm of a schoolmate (she really had as bad a temper as I) my punishment was to master perfectly the entire "Love Chapter." [2] I can even now recall the fear that came upon me when learning some of those searching passages giving the consequences, for example, of telling a lie— this when I had been caught in deception.

---

[1] Prov. 16:32.
[2] I Cor. 13.

When I was about eight—possibly nine—years of age, my parents were puzzled as to how to break me of the habit of slipping out to play leaving tasks unfinished. (I would much rather be playing with a neighbor's baby than drawing beside my father's easel.) One day Mother took me alone and, opening her Bible at the parable of the talents, had me read the whole passage.[3] Though I cannot recall her words, a lasting impression was made upon me as she made vividly plain that some day God would require me to give an account of the talents He had given me. This plan of Mother's in using God's Word did help, for from that time on I tried to apply myself to drawing and other lessons.

One of the most precious memories of those early years was when Mother permitted me to accompany her to Montreal, some four miles west of our home. (My parents had come to Canada three years previously.) The first place visited was the old and interesting Bonsecours Market. In close proximity to the market was the great Notre Dame Cathedral. When finished with her marketing, Mother would say, "Now, child, we will go into the cathedral; I need quiet." Mother was not a Roman Catholic, nor had she any tendency that way. She was the mother of a very large family, and upon her rested the responsibility of making—or trying to make—both ends meet on an artist's uncertain income.[4]

---

[3] Matt. 25:14-30.

[4] John Bell-Smith was the first artist of note to settle in Canada, "The New Country," as it was then called. He sailed from London, England, the summer of 1866 with

Her problems were many. Can we wonder, therefore, that she craved for just such a haven as
was to be found within the quiet, restful cathedral!

As we passed the holy water font just within
the main entrance, where a priest always stood
signing to "dip and cross," Mother would simply
give a slight curtsy and pass on to a seat halfway up to and in sight of the great altar. Never
can I forget the hour, sometimes longer, when
Mother knelt in perfect stillness with face covered. Close beside her I sat, gazing in wonder at
what to my child's fancy was all marvelous
beauty and grandeur. Especially did the wonderful colors of the stained glass windows (the pride
and glory of the Roman Catholic Church in
Canada) appeal to all the artist in me. The "dim
religious light," the quiet and solemn hush of the
place, all had their disciplining influence on my
restless, stormy nature.

Not only on those visits to the cathedral but
in other ways and at other times I came to see
Mother's source of strength was in prayer and in
definitely claiming some promise in the Word.

One of her favorite texts on which to take a
stand was:

> I will go before thee, and make the crooked
>   place straight;
> I will break in pieces the gates of brass,
> and cut in sunder the bars of iron.

two of his sons, the rest of the family following a year later.
A warm reception awaited him in Montreal. A year later
the Canadian Academy of Art was founded with Professor
Bell-Smith as President. This later came to be the present
Royal Canadian Academy.

There were other blessed, molding influences besides Mother. One that stands out most clearly will be mentioned—that of a Sunday school teacher. We children attended the "Cross" Sunday school, so named because it was erected on the site where Jacques Cartier planted the cross on reaching the upper St. Lawrence. It was a mission carried on chiefly by Christian workers who came from the city in a large picnic wagon each Sunday.

No special word or lesson can I recall of this teacher; even her name is forgotten; but all down the years has remained the memory of the sweet fragrance of her Christlike presence. Though but a child, and such an one as I have described, yet if anything, as storm or sickness, prevented me from going to Sunday school, the family did not know what to do with me, I would sob and cry so passionately. They did not know the secret; it was the longing just to watch this teacher's face and feel her tender, loving spirit; this was sufficient. I saw in her what I longed even then desperately to be. (O Sunday school teachers, take courage!)

[5] Then, when I was eleven years of age something happened that seemed to open the door into a new world. Revival meetings were being held in the Cross Sunday school. One evening I was allowed to accompany my oldest sister to the meeting. We sat in one of the front seats.

---

[5] Though this story has been told briefly in *Goforth of China,* it can scarcely be omitted here. If God's word is true, the greatest step one can take is the step "from death unto life."

The leader, Mr. Sandham,[6] took as his text John 3:16 and spoke with great tenderness of the love of God. As he repeated again and again the words, "God loves you," my whole soul responded with gratitude and love. And when he asked all those who wished to take Jesus Christ as their Lord and Master, fear of my sister and others kept me from rising.

That night I sobbed and prayed for hours. At last I promised the Lord that if He would let me live till the next evening, I would confess Him. The following evening, I went to the meeting so full of what I was going to do (I had told no one) that I could afterward remember nothing of what preceded the call for decisions. Mr. Sandham had the invitation to stand only partly said when I was on my feet and remained standing so long that he had to sign for me to sit down! All the while I was standing, my sister was tugging at my dress. On the way home I was told how foolish it was for me to stand as I had, that I was too young to understand. But I knew Christ had received me and that I belonged to Him. In the years to come this definite assurance of acceptance saved me many, many times from despair. And, oh, the joy of that "first love"! Oh, that it had never grown cold!

When I was about twelve years of age my father retired from his profession, and for seven years my sister Gertrude and I accompanied our parents on what might well be termed a migratory

---

[6] Mr. Sandham became founder and editor of *The Faithful Witness,* from which later sprang *The Evangelical Christian.*

life. Among other places lived in temporarily were Toronto and Hamilton. In Hamilton we attended the Church of the Ascension, where I came under the most blessed influence of the Rev. Canon Carmichael and his wife, the latter being my Sunday school teacher. When I told Mrs. Carmichael immediately after my confirmation how I longed to do something for my Saviour, she gave me the ministry of visiting the Old Women's Home and entrusted me with small sums with which to buy little comforts for the old folks. I was very young for such work—scarcely fifteen, but, oh, it was all wonderful, and I was so proud to be *trusted!*

One day a frail, old person asked me to pray with her. I did, but I was so nervous and frightened that I could not hear my own voice! I learned to love those dear, old souls, and my love was fully reciprocated.

The autumn of 1882 found us again settled in Toronto. I at once entered art school. The period of three years that followed was a period of great unrest in my life. I loved my art, for it was born in me, yet there was always the inner, secret longing for definite Christian service. I came to pray daily that a door might be opened for such service.

. . . . . .

Before going further, I would like to give a brief memory of Father.

My father and I were strolling one evening by a country roadside. He was over seventy and had retired from his profession as an artist. It was early summer, and wild violets were in full bloom. Father stopped and plucked a single violet. He remained examining it for so long that I became impatient and said, "Father, dear, do come on." Gently he laid a restraining hand on mine as he said, almost in a tone of awe, "Child, just look at the exquisite beauty of this tiny flower—its color and delicate tracery! Oh, how wonderful it is!" As we started on, he exclaimed, with deep feeling, speaking as if to himself, *"What a wonderful artist God is!"*

I give the following incident as a fitting sequel:

Many years later, when attending the Keswick (New Jersey) Convention, we were on our way to the evening meeting. As we were passing a group of young men evidently engrossed in examining a beautiful water lily, one of them to my surprise stepped forward and placed the lily in my hand. A moment later as they gathered around us, I found myself telling the story of Father and the wild violet. The young men listened with deep interest. I closed with, "If Father could see the work of the Great Artist in that tiny, wild violet, what would he have seen in this perfect and most exquisite lily?"

Months later I received a letter from one of the young men in which he said, "Those words, 'What a wonderful Artist God is,' remained with us, bringing a new and lasting vision of God." The letter enclosed a very lovely photograph of the Keswick lily pond in full bloom.

Two years after returning to Toronto, my father died. Shortly before he passed away, he asked me to sing for him that beautiful hymn,

"Abide with Me." Mother sat beside him as I played and sang through the whole hymn. When the last line of the last verse was reached, *"In life, in death, O Lord, abide with me,"* Father repeated each word softly but distinctly, then lapsed into final unconsciousness.

Mother and my eldest brother, Fred, had given Father their solemn promise that I would be sent to England for training in the Kensington School of Art. In view of this promise Mother's later action may be better and more sympathetically understood.

Little did I dream as we entered the year 1885 how completely the course of my life, as then planned was to change before the year ran out.

Graduation from the art school was to come in May, when a coveted gold medal was to be presented by the Governor General of Canada. One pupil, Miss X, and myself were so far ahead of the others in the class that it was a foregone conclusion that one of us would get the medal. There is little doubt that had I won it I would have been so elated a career as an artist would certainly have followed. But God planned otherwise.

Early in February I was taken ill with inflammatory rheumatism. This was the third serious attack. For days my life hung in the balance. I was only half conscious and unable to move or be moved. Every joint in my body seemed on fire. Some weeks before, I had memorized the hymn, the first verse of which is:

How sweet the name of Jesus sounds
In a believer's ear;

> It soothes his sorrows, heals his wounds,
>   And drives away his fears.

Words fail me to describe what that hymn meant to me through those days of agony. The words, fresh in mind, came without effort. While at times the whole six verses would come as soothing balm, it was the message of the first two lines of the last verse that brought to me the irresistible call to service. The words,

> I would thy boundless love proclaim
>   With every fleeting breath,

seemed burned into my soul. I came out of that valley of suffering determined to pray myself loose from the things that were forcing me to follow other ways than the path of Christian service.

It was then I began to pray that one *wholly yielded up to the Lord and His service might be led to me*.

Graduation time came, and while I was able to attend, I of course failed to win the gold medal, which was awarded to Miss X.

Preparations had begun for my going to England, for I had told no one, not even my mother, of my spiritual struggles and secret hopes, believing it was better to leave the Lord to work out all in His own way. Then, in a truly marvelous way, He brought into my life just what I had asked for, *a man wholly yielded to God and His service*. The story of how Jonathan Goforth and I met and the natural outcome has already been published.[7]

---

[7] *Goforth of China*, chap. III.

As I look back upon that time, the greatest wonder seems to be the *rapidity* with which events took place—the meeting with Mr. O'Brien at St. Peter's, a few days later his invitation to the workers' meeting of the Toronto Mission Union, the introduction of "Jonathan Goforth, our city missionary," and a few days later the never-to-be-forgotten incident of examining the worn Bible. At that meeting, though it was the first I had attended, my name was included in the committee appointed to find a place for and open a branch mission in the east end slums. Mr. Henry O'Brien was chairman, while Jonathan Goforth was also included on the committee. Thus we were co-workers from the beginning.

To my great surprise, Mother's reaction to this slum work was most sympathetic. For weeks all went well. Then one day, as if uneasy, she expressed a wish for Mr. Goforth to come for supper Sunday evening. He came, and Mother liked him. But that evening when I returned from the mission, Mother looked straight at me in a strange way and said, "Rosie, was the moon out tonight?" Everyone in the room had his eyes on me, and my embarrassment was more than I could bear, for I had to acknowledge as I fled that *I did not know!* (Jonathan Goforth had accompanied me home.)

The next morning Mother came to me and said sternly, "This slum work is to cease at once. You are to get ready and leave for England without delay!"

I replied quietly, but firmly, "Mother, it is too

late; I promised Jonathan Goforth last night to be his wife and to go to China!"

Poor Mother! She almost fainted! It is not necessary to give the details of the week that followed. Suffice it to say that Mother gave me the choice of obeying Father's dying wish or leaving home. For six weeks I stayed with a brother in a distant city. Then came a letter from my sister pleading with me to return, as Mother was sobbing day and night and seemed failing fast.

On reaching home, I was shocked at the change in Mother. She would not speak to me and seemed brokenhearted. My distress was now very great. Could it be God's will for me to break my mother's heart? At last, one day as I listened to her pacing her bedroom floor and weeping, I could stand the strain no longer and determined to find out God's will so plainly that I could make no mistake. Going down to the parlor, where the large family Bible rested on a small davenport or desk, I stood for a moment crying to the Lord for some word of light. Then I opened the Bible *at random,* and the first words my eyes lit on were:

> Ye have not chosen me, but I have chosen you, and ordained you, that ye should go and bring forth fruit.[8]

I knew at once God was speaking His will to me through these words, and in an instant the crushing burden was gone. Running to Mother's room, I begged her to hear what I had to say. Unwillingly she unlocked the door and stood while

---

[8] John 15:16.

I told her of my prayer and answer. For a moment only she hesitated. Then with a cry I could never forget, she threw her arms about me, saying, "O my child, I can fight against you, but I dare not fight against God." From that moment till her death eighteen months later Mother's heart was entirely with me in the life I had chosen.

It was a common belief at that time that no one could tell in this life whether or not he was saved. Mother held to this. But after she was gone, the following was found in her diary: "Give me to know, Lord Jesus, before I die, that I am saved." This prayer was answered only as she was passing. It was a glorious scene that seemed to open Heaven to us. Seven children gathered round her bed and as the end drew near, Mother suddenly opened her eyes wide and gazed upwards. Then her expression changed from surprise to joy and then to that of glad welcome, when she raised her arms in greeting, and in a clear voice cried, "Now, evermore Jesus." At this instant a beam of light shone upon her face, and she was gone. Turning to each other, we exclaimed, "Did you see it?" and all, except one who was blind, had seen the shaft of glory.

Many, many times in later years, when facing a group of heathen women, this story of Mother's entrance into the glory land touched the hearts of hopeless women and opened the way for further teaching.

Chapter II

PROOFS OF GOD'S PRESENCE

Open my ears to music: let me
Thrill with Spring's first flutes and drums,
But never let me dare forget
The bitter ballads of the slums.

Patterson Place, a firetrap of an old tenement crowded with the poorest of the poor, was situated in the midst of Toronto's East End slums. The third and top story, used as a dance hall, had recently been raided by the police and was vacant. This we rented for our mission hall, and truly we could not have found a better place for reaching the persons we were after.

The large, low, dirty loft was transformed into an attractive meetingplace. During those days, everything needed—benches, tables, lamps, and even an organ—came in as we knelt in prayer and laid all needs definitely before the Lord. I seemed to be living in a world of miracle.

Strange to say, I was appointed head of the district visitors. Bewildered as to how or where to begin, I turned in desperation to Mrs. Lane, an old, experienced deaconess at the main central mission. This dear woman gave two days in leading me into the slum homes. Practically every door opened to us as Mrs. Lane, with sympathy and love shining in her eyes, sought for entrance. In every home, no matter what the condition of the floor might be, Mrs. Lane knelt and offered a simple, helpful, comforting prayer, and we could feel in the room the hush and stillness of appreciation. Later I determined to do exactly as Mrs. Lane has done; and, oh, in the years that followed, what blessed returns came from every bit of love and sympathy given these struggling, heartbroken, disappointed women!

Space permits of but one story of that time in detail. Indeed it is a wonderful story of what may be termed *blind guidance*.

New Year's Day, 1887, was bitterly cold. Jonathan Goforth and I started for a walk through the Rosedale ravine just north of my home. On reaching Parliament Street, instead of turning northward to the ravine, I stopped short and said, "Jonathan, I feel strangely impressed that we should go south down to the slum district."

He looked at me amazed, and for several moments we stood debating, for he strongly objected, saying very truly that Parliament Street was the last place for a lovers' walk!

At last I said, "Did you ever feel so clearly led to do something that you just *had* to do it?"

To this he replied, "If that is how you feel, let us go south." (But it was a very silent walk!) For almost a mile and half we walked down

Parliament. Then I led the way a block east. By this time I was getting pretty nervous.

Hesitating for a moment, I led on down Sackville Street for over a block, then stopped in front of a small cottage and said, "O Jonathan, don't look at me as if I had gone crazy! Let us knock at this door."

Jonathan, evidently getting anxious, exclaimed, "But why?"

"I don't know," I replied. Now I must say the man of this house was such a drunken fellow I had always avoided visiting his wife af times when he might be in. But at this time I knew of no reason whatever why I should call. We knocked.

The husband opened the door, and on seeing me cried out, with tears running down his face, "Oh, Miss Bell-Smith, God has sent you!"

We found the place like an ice house—no fuel, no fire, no food. The poor wife was lying on a miserable bed with but little over her and seemingly coughing her life away. In the corner of the room lay a dead baby, born a few hours before. Their sad story was quickly told. The man had gone to the city hall for help, but it was closed, it being New Year's Day. Returning to his wife with his last hope of help gone, he sank down by her bedside and joined her in crying to the Lord to send someone to them. *At that very time the strange impelling had come to me.*

The story would not be complete without the following: Forty years later my daughter Ruth (Mrs. D. I. Jeffrey of Indo-China) when on furlough addressed a meeting in the East End Mission Hall. A poor old crippled woman was helped in and seated at the door. She asked that Ruth be brought to her. Then tremblingly she unwrapped a tiny parcel and handed to Ruth a small gold coin worth two dollars and fifty cents, saying, "Give this to your mother and tell her I have never forgotten how she saved my life forty years ago." She had been keeping the coin for that purpose for years.

I hesitate and have hesitated long before writing the following, fearing lest some may misunderstand. But the story touches a chord that runs through most of my life as a struggling overcomer—a climber!

Our beloved mother died in May, 1887. For some time I had felt increasingly that whatever would come to me at her death should be put in trust for a memorial chapel and hospital in China when a permanent station was secured. My reason for this was twofold; first, because of gratitude for what it had cost Mother to give me up. But second (I did not dare tell anyone, not even Jonathan Goforth), I hoped by giving absolutely *all*, even my money, to the Lord I would surely then be worthy of the godly man I was to marry *and become my ideal of what a missionary should be—patient, forbearing, yielding, and easy to get along with!* I knew, as few if any knew, what my artist-temperament meant—it was impulsive, supersensitive, quick-tempered, proud—but why give the whole list of the "little foxes that destroy the vines"? I wanted at any cost to be worthy of Jonathan Goforth. So the

few thousands that came to me were made over
in trust to the church. I kept what I thought was
just sufficient to tide me over till our marriage
a few months later. This led to what seemed
to us both a beautiful seal on our new life.

We were to be married on October 25. For a
month or more, I had been awakening to the
fact that what I had thought would be sufficient
to meet my needs till my wedding day was *not*
sufficient, and I would need fifty dollars more in
order to be married free of debt. I had never
needed to trust for temporal things or money.
It was a time of real testing. I had been much
impressed by Hudson Taylor's simple testimonies
to answered prayer recorded in that wonderful
book, *China's Spiritual Need and Claims*. I resolved, therefore, to ask the Lord for fifty dollars, thinking the while that if I had not faith
enough for this, I was not worthy of being a
missionary. The Lord saw fit to test me to the
utmost, and as the wedding day drew near with
no sign of money, I was sorely tempted to give
someone *just a hint* of my need, but I did not.
Then the evening before the wedding, when
quite a number were gathered in the back parlor,
including Jonathan Goforth, a knock came at
the door. I opened it to find several of my co-
workers from the East End Mission had come
with a beautiful illuminated address. After this
had been presented, a very small purse was
handed to me, which I received, but with the
inward thought, "How strange to give such a
useless thing as this!" When all were gone, I
went back to the friends who were curious to

know what it was all about. Then I held up the purse and said, "Isn't it strange to give such a mite of a thing as this!"

My two hundred forty pound brother Randolph bent back in his chair and laughed so immoderately we thought there would be a crash. He exclaimed, "Why, Rosie, you foolish girl, *open it!*" I did so and found a fifty-dollar gold piece within.

Shortly before we left for China in January, 1888, word reached us of a beautiful twenty-four stop organ being given us by the ladies of Uxbridge. It was, however, too late to go with us, which later seemed quite providential, for had it accompanied us it would most likely have been lost in the fire that destroyed most of our belongings soon after settling in Chefoo.[1]

As I recall those early years in China, my heart warms at the remembrance of what the organ meant to us both. Those who have read the life of my husband will know what an exceedingly strenuous, highstrung life he lived. That which seemed to soothe and rest him more than anything else was when, supper ended, the lights were turned low and he would rest on the sofa for a brief spell before going to the street chapel or other ministry, while I sang and played softly his favorite hymns. Sometimes he would rise and join in the singing.

As I write, a vivid and precious scene, which occurred years later, comes up before me. One Sunday morning in April, warm and bright, we

---

[1] *Goforth of China.*

were singing together by the open window in our home in Changte. The hymn was one my husband loved. The chorus ran:

Angels of Jesus, angels of light,
Singing to welcome the pilgrims of the night.

As he sang, he seemed to forget himself, and with face uplifted and full, unrestrained voice he sang heartily and joyously. Just as the hymn was finished, one of our co-workers appeared at the window and with a look of surprise said, "Why, Goforth, I never knew you had such a voice. We thought you had some great singer over here."

I replied laughingly, for my husband looked rather sheepish, "Yes, he has improved greatly. I tell him he could not carry the tune of 'Jesus Loves Me' correctly when I married him."

My earnest desire in writing these life stories is to help other "climbers," even through my failures, so I give the following incident, which many times has come vividly to mind, always with regret.

On leaving the dreadful "Parthia" [2] at Kobe, on our first voyage to China, we changed to another vessel for Shanghai. There came on board there a missionary and his wife and two little children, one about two years, the other an infant of less than two months. It was noticed on board that the wife, though very frail, seemed to have the entire care of both children, her husband being rarely seen with her.

_____

[2] *Goforth of China.*

One day it was quite rough. As I was descending the winding staircase, holding on to the banister, I met this dear mother ascending to the deck above. One arm held the baby; the other with difficulty kept hold of the older child while steadying herself against the rail. How my heart went out to her in pity! I said to myself, "That cruel husband, to leave her alone with these little children"; *but I did not stretch out a hand to help!* The mother was too intent on trying to save herself from falling even to notice my look of pity.

In years to come, when traveling with my own little ones, how often, when others have helped me while I was in as much need as was she, has the remembrance of my thoughtlessness come vividly to mind. Why did I not help? Perhaps just "cause I didn't think," but it was *a lost opportunity* for we reached port soon after, and I never saw her again.

> I shall pass through this world but once. Any good, therefore, that I can do, or any kindness I can show to any human being, let me do it NOW—for I shall not pass this way again.

As I face my desk this morning, a voice reaches me: "Mother, you surely are not omitting those amusing incidents from that record."

To this I reply, "This which I am writing is not for amusement, and the incidents you refer to would be quite out of place."

"But, Mother," the voice persists, "has God no place for amusement in His plan for His children?"

These words set the thread of memory aglow and there comes the remembrance of that "saving grace of humor" that so characterized my husband all down the years, saving the situation for us numerous times. So I yield, and some incidents that may be considered amusing will find their way into this record.

One experience my dear husband always recalled with keen enjoyment was connected with Chinese donkeys. It occurred a few weeks after our arrival in China. We had moved into our new home following the fire.[3] Our house faced on a narrow but very busy thoroughfare. I was sitting one morning sewing, my husband near by studying with his language teacher, when suddenly the air was rent by what seemed to me bloodcurdling sounds. It was as if an animal were being literally torn to pieces. Each moment the wails and gasps from the poor creature became more heart-rending. I jumped to my feet and, grasping my husband's arm, cried, "Jonathan, those wicked heathen are torturing the poor creature. Oh, go, go and stop them!"

But instead of showing any pity, he kept laughing till the tears ran down his cheeks.

Then as an extra loud and terrible wail came, rising higher and higher, and ending in a death-like gasp—then *silence,* I covered my face and burst into tears, crying out, "O Jonathan, it is dead! I never, never thought you could be so heartless and cruel!"

At this he rose and, putting his arm about

---

[3] *Goforth of China.*

me, controlled himself enough to say, "Why, Rose, do you mean to say you never heard a donkey bray?"

"No," I replied, "But that's not braying!"

"If you don't believe me," he replied, "just look out of the window and you'll find the donkey trotting peacefully along beside its owner."

I ran to the window and saw a dozen donkeys trotting along beside their respective owners, but no sign of even one dead donkey!

Chapter III

LEARNING TO SERVE
BY LOVE

*He taught me to yield up the love of life
for the sake of a LIFE OF LOVE.*
—Mrs. Krumm

When in china about nine months, we moved to an interior mission station, the first step toward North Honan, our ultimate goal. Some of the missionaries at this station were of the very highest type. Among them was Mrs. S., widely known for her success in reaching Chinese women. There were also two young women, twins, who had been but a few months in China. I realized how my husband expected only the highest and best from me as a missionary, and I did not want to fail him or my divine Master. I determined, therefore, to learn something from Mrs. S. that would help me in view of the pioneer life we were facing. Little did I dream what the first lesson was to be.

One day, soon after Mrs. S. returned from a day in the villages, I went over to see her and said, "Mrs. S., I wish you would tell me some of

32

your experiences that might help me in reaching the women."

In answer, she drew me down beside her and said, "I think something I went through today might help you." Then she told me the following story as nearly as I can recall her words:

"This morning I went to a distant village where the Christian women of that section were to meet in a certain house for study. But, as you know, it began to rain, and no outside women came; so I started to read with the Christian woman of the home. We were sitting close together on the kang (a brick platform bed). I had my arm around her as we read. Suddenly she began to cry, saying, 'O Mrs. S., don't let us read any more! My heart is so full I must talk to you.' So I drew her closer while she told me her troubles. The woman went on to say, 'My sister died some months ago, and since then I have had to care for her children as well as my own. Besides all the regular work of meals, sewing and so on, I have to weave cloth late into the night; and for weeks I have had no time for *lice hunting! I and the whole family are just crawling with them: even the bed we are sitting on is just alive!'*"

"O Mrs. S.," I simply gasped; "didn't you jump off the kang?" She replied: "Mrs. Goforth, listen! *I felt like it,* but just as I was about to do so the words flashed through my mind, *'The love of Christ constraineth us;'* [1] and instead *I just drew the woman closer to me.*"

---

[1] II Cor. 5:14.

When I heard this, tears flowed freely as I cried in my heart, "O God, give me such love for my service in China!" Never was the lesson forgotten, and in years to come it was often needed as like experiences were gone through.

At the same station another important lesson was learned—this from the dear twin sisters. At that time home mail came only once a month. One morning as we were studying with our language teacher, an extra bulky foreign mail arrived. At once my husband dismissed the teacher, as it was nearly eleven o'clock, and we gave ourselves up to the enjoyment of at least skimming through our letters.

Remembering that the twins had been anxious about their beloved mother, who was ill in America, I went over to their room to inquire. I found them both studying hard with their language teacher. Expressing my surprise as I pointed to the great heap of mail waiting on a side table, one of them looked up and said hastily, "Yes, yes, we know, *but duty first!* It's study till 12 o'clock."

I turned and closed the door softly behind me, but a lesson had been learned. When I told my husband, he exclaimed, "Well, I am humbled! But we have learned our lesson!"

These young women probably never knew what an important lesson they had taught us through their example in putting first things first.

During the nine months spent at this station, a terrible famine raged throughout the eastern part of the province. For the first time we came to glimpse the horrors of famine. One day a blind beggar refugee led by a little boy about six years of age knelt outside the mission gate. Both were almost dead from exhaustion and starvation. Loving hands led them into the women's hospital, where they were first *cleansed,* then clothed and fed. Gradually, as the woman was able, the following sad story was drawn from her.

Months before, she and her husband with their child had started from their home to beg, as they and all about them were starving. Day by day the husband's strength failed. Then one bitterly cold night they took refuge in a wayside temple. All that night, in front of the idol's shrine, the blind wife knelt beside her dying husband. As the day dawned and the last struggle ceased, the blind woman wakened the child and, grasping her stick, motioned for him to lead her away. As she stood hesitating as to where to turn, there came the remembrance of someone telling of a place far off, a hundred miles away, where lived a man who could give sight to the blind. With desperation born of despair she resolved to reach this man. The suffering endured on the journey can only be imagined. When attempting to tell the story of those days, the poor woman seemed able to recall little else than the ever present dread lest when the gateway of the wonderful man who could give her sight was at last reached, the door would be closed upon them!

The day after reaching the mission gate, Mrs. Ma, the blind woman, was visited by the doctor's wife. "Mrs. Ma," she said, "the doctor wants you to be well fed before he can operate upon you. You must gain strength. Tell me just what you crave for most."

Mrs. Ma could not at first understand. Then, when the meaning dawned upon her, she stretched out her hands, and with a cry in her voice said, "If it is true that I can have what I crave for most, then give me, oh, give me just a little *salt!*"

Just a little salt! What desperation! What agony of want was revealed in that cry! The operation restored the sight of one eye. It was my great joy and privilege to teach Mrs. Ma during her convalescence. My knowledge of the Chinese language at that time was exceedingly limited, but I at least *practiced on her!* From the love she showed to me, I knew she understood the language of love, even through the medium of my poor Chinese. Mrs. Ma became a true Christian and for many years after we left that station served faithfully as matron of the women's hospital. Her son went through all grades of the mission schools and ultimately graduated with honors from Peking Union Medical College.

It was in Dr. and Mrs. Ma's cozy home next to the hospital of which Dr. Ma was in charge that I last saw old Mrs. Ma. She was very old and frail and again quite blind, but happy with her grandchildren about her. Her face radiated peace, and her last words to me were, "We shall meet in Gloryland."

The second major step had been taken. We

had gone farther into the interior and nearer our future field—North Honan.[2] We had just come to a strange city, Linching, and were among strangers.

The following experience may seem to some too sacred for recording, but how may I hope to help other *climbers* if the deep, *furnace* experiences of my life are withheld? So I record it, humbling though it is.

One evening as I lay on a couch beside a paper window through which every sound could be heard, I was drinking to its dregs the cup of sorrow. Little Gertrude, our firstborn, had died that morning. Her father was on his way to a distant station taking the precious remains for burial.

Two Chinese women seated themselves outside the window. I could not help hearing what they said. They were, of course, quite unconscious of my closeness to them. At first they talked with much kindness and sympathy of the event that had just taken place. Then began a most amazing and searching dissection (no better word can express it) of my life and character. We had been told the Chinese were keen judges of character. But this was more. It revealed a surprisingly high conception of a Christian missionary! Incidents with the servants, which I had thought trivial, such as a stern rebuke, a hasty word or gesture, were all given their full value. During the process of dissection they did, however, find some good points. One said, "She speaks our language well and is a

---

[2] *Goforth of China.*

zealous preacher." The other admitted, "And she does love us. *But* it's her impatience, her quick temper!" Then came what struck me as a blow, *"If she only would live more as she preaches!"*

At first I was so angered I could have gone out and given them a piece of my mind, but no, I could not, for it was all *too true*. It was this fact that cut so deeply. Then there came the remembrance of how I had hoped and expected by giving up all, even my money, before leaving Canada for China, my disposition would change. I saw my mistake! As that last hard word was heard, *"If only she would live more as she preaches,"* I fled to my room. I had heard enough. It was useless to stay in China and simply preach Christ and not *live* Christ even before our servants.

Two days later my husband returned to find a doubly crushed and broken wife. Oh, what a comforter and help he was! For many days I walked softly, but the lesson had to be relearned many times. As I look back on that sad, searching experience, I can see clearly it was all a step higher in my life, as I was then just a struggling overcomer, but an overcomer—a climber up life's mountain-side.

The following story of my first effort as street evangelist has always been a treasured memory. It was at least unique!

My husband and Mr. McGillivray, his colleague, on leaving for a tour into North Honan immediately after Gertrude's death, arranged that I stay with Mrs. Perkins, of the American

Board Mission, during their absence. It was in her home Gertrude had died. Our compound was more than a mile distant. The language teacher was there, so each morning, accompanied by my Chinese woman, I walked to this compound for language study. Our way led through a long, narrow street, lined with high brick walls, with heavy gateways opening into the courts beyond.

At first, as I passed along, women and girls kept mostly out of sight, peeping at the strange woman with men's feet. My first step in trying to reach these Chinese sisters was just to smile and nod as I went the full length of the street. Then I learned from the teacher to say correctly, *"Wo yao chieh cho peng-yu* [I want to make friends]." This worked wonders, and before many days women and their children gathered on their doorsteps smiling and bowing. Some finally even asked me to sit down with them. By this time I had learned a very simple chorus in Chinese with a catchy tune. The words ran:

> Come to Jesus; come to Jesus;
> Come to Jesus just now.
> Just now He will save you;
> He will save you just now.

This I would sing to them, which always brought a crowd, and many times there was an encore. Soon they listened to our message, and with the help of my woman, Jesus was preached to them. By the time my husband returned, practically all on the street were my friends. Then we moved to a distant part of the city, and I quite lost sight of them.

Twenty-five years later, on visiting Linching with my husband for special meetings, I was told that for many years the women of that street were inquiring for "the foreign woman who wanted to be their friend."

Twice in the two years spent in Linching, we went down with a precious child to the Borderland. Our precious "Wee Donald," our first-born son, had gone to join his sister Gertrude and the host of other little ones of whom the Saviour has said, "Suffer little children to come unto me."

A few weeks after Donald had left us, we started from Linching with three-months-old Paul in a small houseboat for the journey up the narrow, tortuous Wei River for Chuwang,[3] just inside the long looked for "promised land" of North Honan. Our hearts were lonely and sad, yet joyful in anticipation of at last facing together pioneer service in our own field.

Three days' journey upstream brought us to the landing from which could be seen, far across the fields, the walls and gate of Chuwang. While my husband remained by the boat to see after our things, Mr. McGillivray undertook to escort Paul and myself to the mission. But my escort proved to be utterly unable to compete on foot with the chair-bearers and was soon left far behind. A great crowd could be seen gathering about the town gate. When within hailing distance, the waiting crowds, with howls and yells,

---

[3] *Goforth of China.*

came racing toward us. When the crowds saw a foreign woman and child in the chair, clods of earth were thrown at us from all sides. Little Paul became frenzied with fear, and the chair was again and again almost overturned by the great pressure of the crowd. But the chair-bearers kept their footing and pressed on until the mission gate was reached. Dr. McClure stood holding the gate open ready to let us in. The crowd became so wild and menacing that Dr. McClure seemed at once to sense something must be done to pacify them, so, catching Paul up in his arms as the chair passed through, he held the child high so all could see him. The threatening and yells at once changed to laughs and smiles. (The love for children is a marked characteristic of the Chinese.) A few moments later the gate was closed on a pleased and friendly crowd.

The following incident was, undoubtedly, the most testing in all our missionary experience with my loving Chinese women. I had about decided to withhold this story from these pages, but my daughter urged me to put it in, saying, "Only by giving some pictures of the dark side of mission life can those in the homeland understand the true conditions on the foreign field."

We had been a few months in Chuwang, and the people, as a whole, were still hostile. I had given the baby's *amah* strict instructions never to carry the child outside the gateway, as we had a fairly large court with trees.

My husband and I were to take lunch one day with our neighbor missionary. Just as we were leaving, I turned to wave good-by to the baby, who was in his high chair. His face had such a strange expression on it, and the child was wriggling back and forth so violently, I ran forward, fearing something was hurting him. As I lifted his clothes, I fairly screamed for my husband. *The whole of the child's back was alive with eighty big lice!* (We counted them later.) It took but a few moments to strip the child and put him in a bath.

Some hours later a council of war was held to discover the cause of what we had found. We then learned that, against my orders, the *amah* had taken the child into a Chinese home near by. But this did not explain all. Then a Chinese teacher spoke up and said, "We must tell you the truth. It is not an uncommon thing for a woman who is jealous of another's child to gather all the vermin possible and put it on the little one!" Oh, the horror of it! For days I went about simply loathing the thought of getting in close contact with the women again. But as with Mrs. S., divine love conquered, and from that time I felt a love for the women such as I had never realized before. A miracle? Yes, truly, the miracle of divine grace!

We turn with relief to a very different story from the one just given.

We were passing through one of the very darkest periods of our mission history. The attitude of the people was bitterly hostile and suspicious. If I remember correctly, more than a year passed in Chuwang before the first woman inpatient came. Her case was desperate; otherwise she would not have been brought to us. For weeks, attended by her husband, she lay in the hospital. She was—or had been—a beautiful woman. From the first, her heart seemed ready and waiting for the glorious message we had to give.

One day, to my surprise, as I responded to a timid tap on the door, I found this dear woman standing there, timid and shrinking, uncertain as to whether she would be admitted. She was almost fainting from weakness. Leading her gently in, I placed her on a sofa and had a hot drink brought. Soon these visits became quite regular. As she visited, we talked of the precious truths that were so evidently illuminating her very soul. Half a century has passed since then, but the joy of leading that first woman to Christ still remains. Her favorite hymn was "My home is in heaven; my home is not here." And how she loved to have me sing it while she tried to join in! Many were the lessons she unconsciously taught me of patience and fortitude under great suffering and simple childlike faith and trust. On one of her last visits before returning home, she asked a deep question concerning the Holy Spirit which revealed what wonderful progress she had made in spiritual understanding. Some months later she died, but we knew she had passed away in the joyful hope of meeting her Redeemer.

CHAPTER IV

INCOMPARABLE SERVICE

You do not test the resources of God till you try the impossible.—F. B. Meyer

WE HAD COME at last to facing pioneer living realities. Before us lay the great, heathen city of Changte and around us a vast region with its almost countless towns and villages,[1] and I was the only woman with the message of light for my sisters living in spiritual darkness so dense as to be felt.

On our arrival by cart from Chuwang that first evening, as we entered our three-room Chinese home, I gathered my three children about me and registered a vow that by the grace of God I would do all in my power to take the old, old story to my sisters in that region.

We had come at the time when hordes of women and girls—cotton gleaners—were scouring the countryside. These could be heard as they tore past our gateway, some thirty and forty

[1] *Goforth of China,* chaps. II, VIII, and IX, tells the man's side of the opening of Changte.

at a time. Believing there was safety in numbers, and overcome with curiosity, they would rush into our inner court like untamed animals. They had never seen a foreign woman before and were wild to see the children but would rush off as they had come. This stage quickly passed; then I literally had to *bait* the women to listen by telling them that unless they sat down on the mats provided for them and listened to the story I had to tell, I would not allow them to see inside my home. This plan simply worked wonders. The crowds became so great our court yard from almost daylight till dark resembled a circus.

Things began to disappear in an alarming manner, for while playing the organ ("the mystery box") my back was toward the crowd. Then I had an inspiration, which doubtless saved many a spoon or other article from being slipped up a capacious sleeve. It was simply to turn the organ around, with my seat in the corner; thus I could keep a watchful eye on my audience while playing.

One day my husband taught me a lesson I could never forget. (He was really a wonderful disciplinarian!) The day had been an unusually strenuous one, and I was really very tired. Toward evening, a crowd of women burst through the living room door and came trooping in before I had time to meet them outside. One woman set herself out to make things unpleasant. She was rough and repulsive and—well, just indescribably *filthy*. I paid no attention to her except to treat her as courteously as the rest. But when she put both hands to her nose, saying

loudly, "Oh, these foreign devils, the smell of
their home is unbearable!", my temper rose in a
flash and, turning on her with anger, I said,
"How dare you speak like that? Leave the
room!" The crowd, sensing a "storm," fled. I
heard one say, "That foreign devil woman has a
temper just like ours!"

Now, I had not noticed that the door of my
husband's study was ajar, nor did I know that he
was inside, until, as the last woman disappeared,
the door opened and he came forward, looking
solemn and stern. "Rose, how could you so forget yourself?" he said. "Do you realize that just
one such incident may undo months of self-
sacrificing, loving service?"

"But, Jonathan," I returned, "you don't know
how she—."

But he interrupted, "Yes, I do; I heard all.
You certainly had reason to be annoyed; but
were you *justified*, with all that is hanging in
the balance and God's grace sufficient to keep
you patient?"

As he turned to re-enter his study, he said,
"All I can say is *I am disappointed!"*

Oh, how that last word cut me! I deserved it,
yes, but, oh, I did so want to reach up to the
high ideals he had. A tempestuous time followed
alone in our inner room with my Lord. As I look
back now, it was all just one farther step up the
rocky hillside of life—*just climbing!*

Those very earliest days and weeks at Changte
were indeed times of testing. Often it seemed, at
least to me, all useless, hopeless, like "casting
bread upon the waters." But one little thing

helped me more than I could ever tell. I had a Chinese carpenter make a good-sized blackboard. This I placed on a wall in our livingroom. It was really intended for the children, for the drawing of letters, pictures, and so on. One day when feeling discouraged and in need of help, I opened my Bible and was led (I know) to II Cor. 9:6:

> He which soweth sparingly shall reap also sparingly; and he which soweth bountifully shall reap also bountifully.

So impressed was I with the latter clause I went to the blackboard and printed in large letters, high up out of the children's reach, the words:

HE WHICH SOWETH BOUNTIFULLY
SHALL REAP ALSO BOUNTIFULLY

For more than two years, until our new home was built, this promise remained constantly before me, an ever-present incentive to sow bountifully the Gospel seed, as I have endeavored to picture it, even though it often seemed the seed was being cast on stony ground. The day came, however, when my beloved husband and I were permitted to see bountiful harvests of souls reaped for our Master in that region.

In my husband's life I have told the story of how, in answer to the prayer that seemed like asking for "rain from a clear sky," a truly Spirit-filled helper, Wangfulin, came just when it seemed my husband would break under the strain of those first weeks at Changte.

This "answer" gave me courage to pray for a

Bible woman.[2] Those who know anything of mission work fifty years ago, know that a really helpful Bible woman was far more difficult to secure than a male evangelist. We had as yet no baptized converts, and, as far as I knew, not a single professing Christian woman. But the remarkable way in which Wangfulin had come to us gave me faith to ask and expect the seemingly impossible. I had but a few days to wait, when the answer came.

The Rev. Donald McGillivray was then my husband's sole colleague at Changte. He had charge of the outside touring. One day he came in, calling to me: "Mrs. Goforth, where are you? I've got a full-fledged, ready-made Bible woman for you!" He then told me of coming across, when touring in the foothills of Changte, an elderly widow, who for years had been a leader and preacher in a Buddhist sect. She had become a Christian through a member of the same sect who had heard the Gospel and accepted Christ.

Mr. McGillivray told how this woman, Mrs. Chang, was now as keen to preach the Christian faith as she had been to preach Buddhism. There were difficulties, however, in the way of her coming to me as a Bible woman, but these were surmounted by taking her first as a learner. For years Mrs. Chang was truly a God-sent helper. During the terrible ordeal of 1900, she was faithful almost unto death, being strung up by her thumbs by the Boxers, but saved through the in-

---

[2] *Miracle Lives of China,* chap. II.

tervention of neighbors. She died in 1903, rejoicing in her Saviour.

We had been about nine months in Changte when the weather began to be very hot. Quite unconscious of what it was going to mean to ourselves and the work, we started to use raspberry vinegar, which had come all the way from London, England, at our noon meals. This seemed not so much a luxury as a necessity, for no ice could be obtained and all drinking water had to be boiled. While at dinner we allowed no one inside, but day by day the windows and the open door were banked with faces keenly watching. Fear, even terror, seemed written on some faces. This went on for several weeks, when a hint came to us of a report being widely circulated that we could be seen day by day drinking the blood of children we had killed. Of course no more raspberry vinegar appeared, but, oh, the horror of it!

At last we moved into our comfortable semi-foreign home. My husband seemed to be walking on air, he was so happy to find the new home proving a help and not a hindrance to the spread of the Gospel, for we continued to keep open house.

As a concession to Chinese ideas, the veranda, running the full length of the house, had been made the usual narrow width. Two persons walking together had to have one keep slightly behind the other or bumps on posts would follow. One evening my husband and I were taking a brief constitutional on the veranda before his leaving for the street chapel. He kept stepping out so fast and so vigorously that I became quite out of breath trying to keep pace with him. At last I exclaimed, "Jonathan, what are you thinking of? I can't keep up with you."

At once he slackened his pace and said, with a look of joy, "Why, Rose, I was thinking what a glorious work this is. Do you know, *I would not change places with a millionnaire*—no, not with Rockefeller himself."

To this my heart thrilled a very joyous response.

Yet to be quite truthful, the method we had adopted was sometimes exceedingly testing to patience and endurance, at least to me as the mother of several small children. Sometimes I just prayed for a rainy day, so women would not come, and I could have a chance to make headway with the children's sewing and lessons. Sometimes women appeared in bands any time almost from daylight till dark. I will give one picture that must speak for itself why, at times, the way seemed *HARD*. It is but a typical case in many.

One day, when in the midst of cutting out a child's dress, with material, scissors, etc., spread on the dining table, a crowd of women burst into the room. For a little while all was utter confusion, the women struggling with each other to get at the baby in the *amah's* arms. (I always seemed to have a baby in arms those days.) By use of a little tact and urging, I soon had them all seated on the rugs, which they preferred to chairs. The promise that all would be shown everything they wished to see if they kept quiet and listened, proved then and many times later, a valuable *bait*. A half-hour, or as long as they would listen, I preached Christ to them; then the promise had to be kept. Nothing escaped their curious eyes. Beds had to be turned up, the sewing machine run and the organ played. But the high mark of interest was in kitchen and cellar; though some women were too frightened to enter the latter. When satisfied, all hurried away as they had come. Tired, and questioning, "Is it worth while?" I returned to my work, to find scissors and most of the material gone; not enough left to finish the dress! Provoking? Exceedingly provoking! But there is always a price to pay for what is worthwhile.

One little, illuminating incident of this period I can never forget. Our beautiful, golden-haired Florence was so fond of dolls that in the course of her eight years of life a regular little family had gathered about her. One of her favorite ways of playing with them was to place all in a row, just inside a bed, with the heads peeping above the clothes. Some had faces very lifelike: some could sleep!

One day while I was leading a crowd of women through the house, some rushed ahead into the bedroom. One glance at the dolls caused them to shriek in terror and run as for their lives. Those behind pressed forward to learn the cause of the alarm, and on catching sight of the dolls, a panic seized them. They fairly trod on each other in their haste to get out. The report was widely circulated that we kidnapped children. These women no doubt added greatly to this report, for had they not seen a whole row of them?

But times were changing. The promise, "He which soweth bountifully shall also reap bountifully," was being fulfilled. Women came more and more quietly to sit and listen—yes, and learn and accept the wonderful message of a Saviour from sin, who was able to give them hope, eternal hope. Oh, it was wonderful to see interest change to hope, and hope to wonder and joy when I was dealing with women who had never heard a word, a hint of any hope for the future. Often I wished that women in the homeland could see such evidence of the transforming power of the Gospel and experience the joy of leading a soul out of darkness to the One who alone is the Light of the world. How it cheered one to have women come again and again and say, "Tell us more about the One who can help us!"

The following is a glimpse of *how,* or perhaps *why,* the work grew so surprisingly. About ten miles to the south of Changte lay the large farming village of Takwanchwang. The leading and most prosperous farmer of that region appeared one day with the request that Dr. Goforth lead him through our home as I did the women. Everything was examined as far as the kitchen. Then Mr. Wang, the farmer, said, "Isn't there anything more?"

"Well, no," was the reply; "only the cellar."

"Cellar!" exclaimed the farmer. "Why, that is what I came to see most of all." Down they went. Coal and book boxes—everything was examined, my husband helping in the search! Then, when satisfied that nothing had escaped him, Mr. Wang turned to Dr. Goforth with a look of utter amazement, saying, "Oh, but we Chinese are liars! My neighbors told me they had seen with their own eyes crocks of children's flesh salted down in the cellar! It's that which has kept me from coming to you before."

A few days later this man again turned up leading a band of the chief men of his village. With a triumphant look in his eyes, Mr. Wang led as he had been led. On reaching the cellar, he cried, "Look now; look, I say. Dig deep into the coal. Search and see if you can find even one dead baby. Oh, you liars, to tell me you had seen them!" Then off to the city the men were taken, where Mr. Wang treated them all to a grand feast.

This was not all. A few days later a farmer's four-wheeled wagon appeared, loaded to the limit with women, all whom Mr. Wang could coax to come. They were led through the same process of enlightenment. All were frightened and timid till they returned from the cellar; then they were joking and laughing and even willing to partake of the tea and refreshments I had provided for them, though before they had been too frightened to taste anything lest they be bewitched. These women also were treated to a dinner by Mr. Wang. Is it much wonder Takwanchwang became the first self-supporting outstation? Many are the happy memories of visits to that center!

But enough has been written of that early period. Clouds, dark and threatening, were fast

gathering. Uncertainty, suspense, alarming rumors, unrest among the people, threats of attacks
by organized bands, all culminated in sickening
dread of what the future might bring.

Then the beginning of that hurricane of horrors came.

On June 19, 1900, our darling seven-year-old,
beautiful, gentle, sunny Florence, lay dying.
Gently my husband had insisted on my leaving
the room before the end came.

As I paced up and down under the starlit sky,
wails of the people praying to their gods for rain
could be heard on all sides, for the sky had been
as brass for many months, and cruel famine was
at the door. Fear, heart-gripping fear, seemed
pressing upon one from all sides. And Florence!
How could I see even a ray of light in the darkness? As I cried aloud with my hands clasped
heavenward, "O God, O Lord Jesus, why?
Why?" there came the answer, "What I do thou
knowest not now; but thou shalt know hereafter." And again, as if written in the starlit sky,
"The Lord Reigneth." Then the presence of the
Lord became very near in comforting, sustaining
power, and I was ready for the word that soon
came. Our darling's sufferings were ended.

The story of our escape with its record of repeated and miraculous deliverances, has already
been told in my husband's life.[3]

There is an experience I withheld from that
account as it concerned more particularly myself

---

[3] *Goforth of China,* chap. X.

and the children. This experience meant much to me, revealing as it did the tender compassion of the Lord for His child in desperate need; I feel it should be given here.

We had reached Shanghai, which we found crowded with refugees. The only place found for us to spend the ten days before our steamer sailed was an empty house in which a few pieces of absolutely necessary furniture had been placed. My husband and Paul were able to buy some ready-made clothes and I had succeeded with great difficulty in having *one* dress made by a Chinese tailor. But the other three children! They were in rags given by the Chinese on the journey. How could I, without materials, without a machine, get an outfit made for even one, and the ocean voyage just ahead! Alone with the baby one morning I cast myself down by the little one and cried again and again to the Lord to send someone to help me. My distress was great. Help I must have, but I knew no one to whom I could turn. Then suddenly, *while I was praying*, the doorbell rang. On opening the door I found two women outside. They introduced themselves and told of having seen our names among those of the refugees. They were in charge of a Chinese girls' school, but on account of the Boxer troubles, all the girls had been sent home. They then said, "We have nothing to do and thought you may need help." Scarcely able to speak, I told them rapidly my story; how I was on my knees pleading for help when they rang the bell. A few moments followed in which we stood clasping hands, weeping, just too full for speech. Then they went away to get materials, for there was no time to lose.

In a very short time, they returned with a pile of materials of from three- to five-yard lengths. I cut out and gave directions for a number of garments. The women took all away and, with the help of some friends, made practically everything needed *except for the baby,* who in the rush of getting others provided for, *was forgotten!* The day we sailed, I gathered a quantity of material together, planning to make the most necessary things for him on board ship. Then came the most beautiful proof of all of God's overshadowing care.

We had been passing through the Inland Sea and were nearing Yokohama. I had been trying my utmost to get some necessary things ready for baby W., but my hands trembled so I could scarcely hold the needle. I struggled on, realizing my strength was going, but kept sewing till I could no longer see the needle. Rising, I folded the work and, going down to the cabin, put it quietly, numbly into the trunk, saying, "Lord, I have done all I can. I can do no more. As you provided for the others, do so now for baby." I then went on deck and lay down on a long chair exhausted. How long I lay there I do not know, but suddenly someone touched me and said, "There's a large bundle come off the lighter for you: it is in your cabin." Dazed at first, I could not take it in. Then it flashed into my mind, "It's the answer!"

In the cabin, I found a letter attached to the bundle from Mrs. O. E., of the China Inland

Mission, whose husband was at that time risking his life in China, seeking to bring out to safety women of the mission who were in peril. The letter stated that her little son, the same age as my baby, had died some months before and she felt it laid upon her to send me, for my child, his outfit. I opened the bundle to find not only a most beautiful, complete outfit for my little one, but also many things I needed for myself and the other children. It was indeed one of the Lord's exceedingly abundant answers. Is it any wonder that those words written so long ago by the psalmist have always had a deep thrill of response in my heart?

I love the Lord, because he hath heard my voice and my supplications.

Because he hath inclined his ear unto me, therefore will I call upon him as long as I live.—Ps. 116:1-2.

CHAPTER V

A MOTHER'S TRAGIC JOURNEY

From silken self, O Captain free
Thy soldier, who would follow Thee:
From subtle love of softening things,
From easy choices, weakenings,
From all that dims Thy Calvary,
O Lamb of God, deliver me.
—Amy Carmichael

Following the boxer uprising, my husband returned to China in the autumn of 1901. Nine months later, toward the end of June, all preparations were complete for myself and five children (the eldest eleven years, the youngest ten months old) to leave for China on the first of July. A few days previously, the papers were full of the cruel massacre of the Stewart family and others with them. Some, fearing a fresh uprising in China, had written our secretary, Dr. R. P. McKay, urging that we be detained, but I felt very definitely we should keep to our original plans.

The following story of our two months' journey, during which I learned what it meant to be

58

carried through each day by divine enabling, is given here with the hope it may help severely tried mothers and perhaps others.

On July 1, a large party gathered at the Union Station to see us off. We were to travel tourist, as more convenient with so many children. As the train was about to start, I heard ominous sounds from the farther end of the car. Listening, as a hand gripped mine through the window, I had just time to exclaim, "Whooping cough!", and we were off.

My heart sank, on turning from the window to find the car so crowded. We had to have three in a seat, and at one end of the car was a party of immigrants, more than one of whose children were, at that very moment, *very evidently* in the throes of whooping cough!

It will be impossible to give the details of each day of the journey. I can write but a brief record of outstanding facts and leave the reader to use some imagination in reading between the lines.

The great heat, combined with car congestion, made the journey to Winnipeg trying even to those without children. On reaching that city, we found all tracks in the vicinity of the station blocked with delayed trains. Reports were rife of serious damage, through floods, to the railway ahead. But no one could learn anything definite. Many hours of waiting followed; then the forward movement began, though slowly, and continued with intermittent delays, till we reached Calgary. Here we were told to leave the car and be prepared for a wait of several days—possibly a week, as forty miles (as I now remember) of track had been washed out by floods.

I shall not attempt to describe the scramble and rush for hotels that followed. It was a case of everyone for himself. How could I, with five helpless children, not to speak of bundles and baggage, compete in *time* with the crowds? Oh, how I kept crying in my heart to the Lord to undertake for us! And He did, for it seemed to me nothing short of a miracle when I at last found myself in a fine, large, cool room in the hotel, with not a child or piece of baggage missing!

Later another passenger came to share the room with myself and four children, Paul having been accommodated elsewhere. The first few days were indeed a welcome time of rest. Then rumors floated about, changing with every hour! Handbags were packed and unpacked several times a day. At last one morning someone rushed in to say several packed trains had already gone and the last one would leave in half an hour!

"Rush" is a word quite inadequate to describe what followed. On reaching the station with babies and baggage, I found the train about to start and so crowded that men were standing on the lowest step. I pleaded frantically that room be made for us. At first the answer from a dozen or more was, "Impossible." Then several kind-hearted ones undertook by squeezing and pushing to make room for us. The children were hauled up and a place made on the arm of a seat for me, where I could hold baby Constance. I had not the least idea what had become of the baggage! The heat of the packed car was almost suffocating. We traveled this way several hours; then the train stopped at a place where the bridge had sunk in the middle. Rough planks had been placed over the tracks, some dangerously wide apart. We were told to leave the train and cross the bridge, that trains were waiting at the farther end. Considering the number of children I had, and the work of gathering up my baggage from various parts of the car, it is little wonder that by the time we were gathered outside all the others had gone on ahead. Realizing how futile it would be to attempt to cross without assistance, I begged a railway official for help. He looked at us steadily for a few moments, taking all in—children, baggage, and my distressed self. Then, turning to a group of navvies by the tracks, he called in no uncertain manner, "Take this woman and her kids across the bridge!"

So we passed over to the other side, only to find the train gone. About twenty or more other passengers left behind like ourselves were seated on logs. We joined these people and for several hours waited there until a train came. My troubles would have seemed then to be over, but evident symptoms had appeared that at least three of the children—Ruth, Wallace, and Constance —had contracted whooping cough. It was not until we reached Vancouver, however, that the real whoops began. So many children, whose parents were booked for the same steamer, had contracted the whooping cough that the usual rule forbidding any with infectious disease on board was waived and all were allowed to sail.

The boat had a full passenger list; I found four of the children and myself allotted to one small cabin. There was absolutely no other plan but to put Helen on the top berth, Ruth and Wallace below, baby Constance on the short settee, and myself on the floor. Only in this way could I reach the children at night when a spasm of whooping came. Needless to say, prolonged, restful sleep was impossible. On the sixth day out I collapsed! The ship's doctor ordered complete rest. The children were taken care of for a day; then I gathered them about me and trusted the Lord to carry me through. Through the days that followed till Japan was reached, and on through the fierce heat of the Inland Sea, I learned what it meant to "go in the strength of the Lord God." [1] Hope and courage came, too, as I thought of the dear father, so soon to meet us on our arrival in Shanghai.

When the ship dropped anchor at the mouth of the great Yangtze River, and the lighter from Shanghai drew near, the children were worked up to the highest pitch of excitement to see who could catch sight of Father first. But, oh, the disappointment when all meeting friends among the other passengers had come aboard, but *no Father!* Then came the general embarking on to the lighter. The journey upstream was so slow it was well on to 1 A.M. when the bund of Shanghai was reached. Leaving the children on the

---

[1] Psalm 71:16.

upper deck, out of the crush, I took my stand by the gangway so as to meet my husband as he came aboard. But just as the wharf was reached, through darkness, appeared the face of Mr. X. of the home where we were to stay. Handing me a telegram over the side of the lighter he said: "Keep up your courage, Mrs. Goforth; there's rather bad news!" Of course I at once thought the worst—that my husband was dead; and for a moment or two all went black as I steadied myself by the rail. The telegram, however, read: "Goforth typhoid Changte," which meant that my husband was lying ill of typhoid fever over one thousand miles away, in our interior station of Changte and in the intense heat of midsummer. Mr. X. was asked to get the best nurse for the children as quickly as possible, for I realized that the breaking point was not far off.

On our way to the home, which we reached about 2:00 A.M., we were told that cholera was raging in the foreign settlement as well as in the native city, the death toll reaching over fifty a day.

As the door closed on the double room allotted to us, I became aware of an overpowering odor! Not till the children were settled in their beds did I discover this came from the bed I was to occupy. What was discovered cannot be described. I turned deathly sick. Staggering to the outside balcony, I threw myself on the boards, pressing my face as close as possible to the rails. There I fell asleep from utter exhaustion. Awakened by the sun, I at once sought the housekeeper, who, on hearing what I had found, turned pale, saying, "Oh, those awful Chinese boys (male servants); I trusted them to prepare your room!" It was not till sometime later I learned a death had taken place there shortly before we arrived.

Mr. X.—and, indeed, everyone—was wonderfully kind. For days I lay in a quiet, comparatively cool, private sitting room. At first my strength was spent in trying to keep the couch and myself from going through the floor. Then, as promise after promise from God's wonderful Word was laid hold on, peace came; I rested and learnt by experience the truth of these words: "Underneath are the everlasting arms." [2]

Later, the telling of this experience helped others suffering from one of the most terrible of physical ills—nervous exhaustion or prostration.

For a week we remained in Shanghai, trying in vain to get word from Changte. Then came the journey by coast steamer to Tientsin, via Chefoo, where Paul and Helen were to be left at the China Inland Mission schools. On our vessel reaching Chefoo, Mr. Murray, of the schools, came aboard for Paul and Helen, but on learning that the other children had whooping cough, he said that Paul and Helen must go through a period of quarantine before being admitted. Just then Mrs. Hunter Corbett came aboard and saved the situation by offering to take charge of them during the quarantine period. The trunk containing Helen and Ruth's winter clothes was brought on deck (Ruth, too, was to

---

[2] Deut. 33:27.

have been left at the schools) for division of the clothes. But on opening the trunk, we found it to be a seething mass of black mold. The only possible explanation for this was that the trunk must have been dropped into water when crossing the flooded region on the Canada overland journey. As two-thirds of the contents were ruined, they were thrown overboard. Mrs. Corbett again came to the rescue, promising to oversee the making of a new winter outfit for Helen. In less than an hour we were on our way northward.

The brief but exceedingly hard experience when getting from the steamer to the train at Tako resembled somewhat the rush from train to hotel at Calgary. We fully expected on reaching Tientsin that mail would be there telling of my husband's condition, but again came sickening disappointment. We did not know the cause till later. The Chinese postmaster at Peking kept sending all mail addressed "Goforth" back to Changte whether to or from that station!

For almost a month, through August, we remained in Tientsin, each day expecting and hoping for some word from Changte, but each day brought only silence. Then one day, without warning, the dear Father appeared! Just a mere shadow of himself, but himself. All the strain and hardness of the journey were forgotten in the reunion.

Chapter VI

REACHING FORTH

Patience means restraining blame;
Patience means enduring shame;
Patience means in fiercest flame,
Standing still.—Selected

O<small>N</small> RETURNING TO CHINA after the tragic journey of which I have just written, I thought my consecration to God was entire. Gratitude for our marvelous deliverance alone would lead to this. But how little we know our own hearts! Frequently during the course of that journey I found myself planning my future. I decided that henceforth the women's work at our station would be left entirely in the hands of the other women missionaries, so I could devote myself to home and children. But God planned otherwise. The story of the bitter struggle for my own way —how it needed the furnace to make me yield; how only at the death of our precious one-year-old Constance did the vision of the Father's love break my hard heart and cause me to surrender my will to His—is told so fully in *Goforth of China* it need not be repeated here.[1] Suffice it to

---

[1] *Goforth of China,* chap. XI.

say a new life of obedience and of an ever widening horizon began for me.

Instead of settling down in our comfortable home at Changte, I at once began preparations for the new life of itinerating with my husband. In the years that followed, weeks, even months at a time, were given to aggressive evangelism in the larger centers of our field. It was indeed a wonderful life in which to learn what a faithful Lord could and would do when all human props failed. It was not, by any means, an easy life— this traveling about from place to place with our remaining children, in constant contact with people who had no idea of sanitation, living in native compounds. But as I now recall those years, they seem among the happiest and certainly the most fruitful of my life. True, there were times when I was tempted to give up, but the Lord was ever present to encourage and sustain; and, oh, how much I owed to my patient, faithful, ever cheerful husband.

The following incident may be enlightening as one of the *testing times!*

The summer was ending with a wave of extreme heat the day my husband and I with two children started out for our autumn touring, beginning at Tzuchou, an important center about twenty miles up the railway line. We were all clad in the lightest garments, there being no sign of change of weather. My husband had sent word ahead to the evangelist for coolies to meet us at the railway station, which was out in the open country, the mission compound being some two miles distant.

When we were about a quarter of an hour from Tzuchou, the sky became suddenly darkened by dense clouds from the north. Just as the train reached the station, the storm in all its fury broke upon us with blinding clouds of dust and sand. We could scarcely see inches away and with great difficulty reached the shelter of the station, which would soon be closed. No evangelist or coolies were in sight. Our letter had evidently miscarried. There was nothing for us to do but to face the long walk over rough, plowed fields leaving our "boy" (servant) to watch the baggage. Dr. Goforth led the way, carrying the heavier child, while the *amah* and I followed as best we could with the younger one. Darkness had set in. The wind, with rain, seemed unabated. Stumbling, sometimes falling, over the hard clods of earth, trying to keep my husband in sight, shivering with cold from the sudden drop in temperature of over thirty degrees, the *amah* and I, while sharing the burden of the child, groaned and wept all the way. Again and again I vowed nothing, no nothing could, or would, make me go out with the children again!

At last we reached the mission, or rented Chinese compound. No time was lost in getting coolies off for our baggage. In the meantime, Chinese bread and a tin of sweetened, condensed milk were secured. (How often have I been thankful that these could usually be had from native stores!) With some boiling water soon all were warming up with bowls of hot bread and milk. On the arrival of our baggage, bedding was spread on the brick, platform beds, and the children were soon asleep. But still I kept vowing to myself that this touring life must cease.

The following morning women began to pour in. One fine Christian woman, with a bright, shining face came in saying, "Mrs. Goforth, you don't know what a help it is to us all, your coming out as you do with your children. Everyone knows what a home and comforts you give up just for the sake of bringing the good news to us women."

Oh, how my heart thrilled as she spoke! Little did she know what her words meant to me. The vowing of the night before vanished. Joy filled my heart, and I knew that the Lord understood. He had borne wonderfully with my faintheartedness. Many times the following words would come to me:

> Like as a father pitieth his children, so the Lord pitieth them that fear him.[2]

It was a wonderful life! Sometimes when letters would reach us from the homeland expressing pity for us, how my husband would laugh as I read them to him! "Pity," he would say, "why this is the most glorious life possible!" Yes, it was indeed!

But it was not all giving out. Often lessons of deepest import were learned from some of the humblest Christians. Just one example of this:

At a certain center frequently visited was a middle-aged woman noted for her violent ungovernable temper. She was utterly ignorant and

---

[2] Ps. 103:13.

what might be termed *stupid*. This woman received Christ into her life. Some months later,
when visiting the village, I asked her if she was
doing anything for her Saviour.

In answer, she drew from her sleeve a cate-
chism (a little booklet of some thirty pages giving in clear form the essentials of the Christian
faith). She said, "Lady, I'm very stupid and
can't learn to read, so I just take this book with
me wherever I go, into all the village homes, and
I get those who can read to read it. But, lady,
they all knew of my temper, and because of the
change in me—*that I love everyone now,* they
all want to read and learn what has made the
change in me!"

The following incident has always seemed to
me one of the saddest of those touring years:

My husband and I were on our way to a certain large center—an important outstation. It
was Saturday, and we were due to begin a series
of meetings the following day. When about halfway, we had to stop at a village to water the animals. We women—myself and the Bible women
—were perched on a large, farm cart loaded high
with baggage. Dr. Goforth walked with the
evangelists, taking his turn with them in an oc-
casional lift by the cart.

Just as we stopped, a woman came running
up to the side of the cart. Taking hold of my
hand, and peering closely into my face, she cried:
"Is it Miss Pyke? No, oh, no, it is not! I was in
the hospital at Changte for several months, and
Miss Pyke taught me how to pray. I've tried to
tell my neighbors [by this time quite a crowd

had gathered about us], but I don't know how. All I can do is to put my hands together and say, 'Jesus, Saviour, forgive my sins; pity me; cleanse my heart and save me.' Oh, do, do tell my neighbors quickly."

I tried to tell, but my voice broke, so I had to sign to Mrs. Wang, my Bible woman, to speak. I had recovered enough to say only a few words when the call came for us to go on. The poor woman tried, almost frantically, to persuade our men to stop "just one night." The villagers joined in pleading, "We want to hear." *But we had to go on!* We never saw those dear people again, for we left the Changte field soon after.

The chief reason I had fought so hard against taking the children out on our country tours was the fear lest they might contract disease, for epidemics of smallpox, diphtheria, and scarlet fever were common among the people, and there was no way of avoiding contact. Later, when that life was a thing of the past, I could say, with praise to God, that not one of the children had contracted an infectious disease as a result of that life. Nevertheless there were times when my faith was tested sorely. The following story is given, not only as an illustration of this but also because it lifts the veil on this touring life.

My husband had tried for many months to get an opening in an important center, but in vain. Then came a letter from the evangelist of that region saying that a compound had been secured, but he hinted it was scarcely fit for a woman and children. But I insisted on us all going. My faith was very strong and trustful *till we reached the place;* then the real test came!

A long day's journey in a springless cart over execrable roads brought us to our new home. The first court was occupied by evangelists and other men; then came the women's court—unspeakably filthy; but, on reaching the third court, where we were to live, we found the worst conditions ever met with, before or later.

A number of great *kangs*—open crocks containing from thirty to forty gallons—lined two sides of the court. These were filled with some stuff that had been fermenting for months and emitted breathtaking odors. But, worse still, a pigsty surrounded two-thirds of the two-room building set apart for us. We had three children with us. The town was the most important pottery center of North China; a number of great kilns surrounded the place. The fuel used for burning the pottery was a fine coal dust that gave out strong gas. The evening we arrived, there was no wind to carry the gas away, and the air was stifling.

My heart just sank as I thought of the children living in such a place for ten days. That night, when my husband had gone to the evening meeting and the children were asleep, I noticed the youngest very restless and feverish. A feeling of simple panic seized me. Throwing myself down on my knees beside him, I prayed in agony to the Lord to keep my child from harm. I committed the little one to Him, but, oh, so tremblingly. Then worn out, I fell asleep. Wakened two hours later by my husband's return, I at once felt the child's head. It was almost cool, and the restlessness was gone. The following morning the child was quite normal and frisky as ever. All through the days that followed, my weak faith kept me watching the children fearfully for any sign of fever, but all were kept well. They seemed to enjoy everything as if it were a royal picnic.

I should perhaps add that while our pioneering in this center was for years very hard and trying, known for its bitter anti-foreign, anti-Christian spirit, yet the day came when the leading people of this place joined in giving us a truly wonderful welcome. They pushed back into obscurity the gods in one of their largest temples, and cleaned and fixed over for our use the part that had been occupied by them.

Long ago, I read somewhere the following: "Before he can be greatly used, a missionary must go through a 'missionary baptism.'" The experience I relate has always seemed to me, at least, akin to this.

I had been for some time in close touch daily with many heathen women, trying to make known to them the glorious news of life beyond and of the One who alone can open the door to that life.

One day, when the crowd had gone, an over-powering mental agony came as I thought of the multitudes by whom we were surrounded who had never heard the Gospel and most of whom never would know. I paced my room, crying to God from my very soul, "Is there not some light, some way out of the darkness?" Words fail me to record what those hours of soul struggle meant.

Then clearly came the message: "Shall not the Judge of all the earth do right?" [3] "What I do thou knowest not now; but thou shalt know hereafter." [4] And clearly, too, came the message, "Just leave all with Me. Your part is to tell out My plan of love."

A great peace came. Yes, mine was to tell out the glorious message of love and eternal hope. From that time just telling the story as to little children became joyous, not irksome.

Often, oh, often, have I wished the homeland supporters could have stood behind me as I talked to a crowd of women who had never till then heard of a Saviour friend. How I wished they could witness for themselves the soul's awakening in hopeless eyes. The saddest part of it is that so many who would have heard the good news gladly never had a chance to hear.

When looking over some old letters, I came across a small, much worn notebook used many years ago when traveling by chair in South China. On the inside of the cover, written in pencil, evidently when on the road, was recorded an incident, long ago forgotten. Although out of place in time, it fits in spirit with what I have just recorded:

Traveling by chair through a poverty-stricken district in China, where old men and children could be seen by the roadside digging out roots of grass and weeds for fuel, I felt greatly oppressed by the barrenness and hope-

---

[3] Gen. 18:25.
[4] John 13:7.

lessness that seemed to prevail everywhere. Suddenly there was thrown into my chair a beautiful bunch of sweet, fresh, wild violets.

"Oh," I exclaimed, "where did you get these?"

"Why, look," was the reply of my husband, who had been walking beside my chair, "the road is full of them!" And so it was, with my dim-visioned eyes, engrossed in bemoaning the barrenness, I had failed to see the messengers of God whose beautiful faces were and had been peeping at me all the way, as if to say, "Look at me, and me, and me! See how good and how beautiful a God we have!" As I turned to the violets in my hands and found the same exquisite beauty and delicate coloring as if they had come from a favorite homeland hedge, I felt the presence of our omnipotent Lord and was comforted. He, the great Artist, held the key to the problem of suffering and all its mystery.

A devoted Christian missionary, Mrs. S., was holding a series of special meetings for our Christian women at Changte. On one occasion, this dear woman, who had no children, told me that I could never have the peace and joy I longed for unless I rose early and spent from one to two hours with the Lord in prayer and Bible study.

I longed intensely for God's best—for all He could give me, not only to help me live the true, Christian life but also for peace and rest of soul. So I determined to do what Mrs. S. had advised.

The following morning, about half-past five o'clock, I slipped as noiselessly as possible out of bed. (My husband had already gone to his study.) I had taken only a step or two when first

one and then another little head bobbed up; then
came calls of "Mother, is it time to get up?"

"Hush, hush, no, no," I whispered as I went
back, but too late; baby had wakened! So, of
course, the morning circus began an hour too
soon.

But I did not give up easily. Morning after
morning I tried rising early for the morning
watch, but always with the same result. So I went
back to the old way of just praying quietly—too
often just sleeping! Oh, how I envied my husband, who could have an hour or more of unin-
terrupted Bible study while I could not. This led
me to form the habit of memorizing Scripture,
which became an untold blessing to me. I took
advantage of odd opportunities on cart, train, or
when dressing, always to have a Bible or Testament at hand so that in the early mornings I
could recall precious promises and passages of
Scripture.

The following is the most notable incident
connected with this habit of memorizing Scripture. I give it, for, judging by the effect it has had
upon men and women to whom I have told this
story, it touches a vital point in the relation of
husband and wife. It certainly brought to my
husband and myself a lesson never forgotten.

Our children were all away at school. We were
together carrying on aggressive evangelism at a
distant outstation. The room given to us was dark
and damp, with the usual mud floor. The weather
had turned cold, and there was no place where
one could get warm. I caught a cold. It was not a
severe one, but enough to make me rather miser-

able. The third or fourth day, when the meetings were in full swing and my organ was taking an attracting part, I became possessed by a great longing to visit my dearly loved friend, Miss H., living at the Weihuifu Station, some hours' run south on the railway. But when I told my husband what I had in mind, he strongly objected and urged against my going. I would not listen, even when he said my going would break up at least the women's work. But I was determined to go and ordered the cart for the trip to the railway. As the cart started and I saw my husband's sad, disappointed, white face, I would have stopped, but I wanted to show him I must have my way *sometimes!*

Oh, what a miserable time I had till my friend's home in Weihuifu was reached! Miss H. gave one glance at my face and exclaimed: "Whatever is the matter, Mrs. Goforth! Are you ill?"

My only answer was to break down sobbing. Of course I could not tell her *why*. Miss H. insisted on putting me to bed, saying I was ill! She made me promise to remain there until after breakfast.

The following morning, while waiting for breakfast, I opened my Testament and started to memorize, as usual, my three verses. Now it happened I was at that time memorizing the Epistle to the Ephesians and had reached the fifth chapter down to the twenty-first verse. The twenty-second, the first of the three to be memorized that morning, read: *"Wives, submit yourselves unto your husbands as unto the Lord."*

I was, to say the least, startled! Somehow I bravely managed to get this memorized. Then going on to the twenty-third verse, I was faced by these words: "For the husband is the head of the wife, even as Christ is the head of the church: and he is the saviour of the body."

For a moment a feeling of resentment, even anger, arose. I could not treat this word as a woman once did, putting it aside with the remark: "That is where Paul and I differ." I believed the Epistle to the Ephesians was inspired, if any portion of Scripture was. How could I dare cut out this one part to which I was unwilling to submit? How I managed to memorize that twenty-third verse I do not know, for all the while a desperate mental struggle was on. Then came the twenty-fourth verse: "Therefore as the church is subject unto Christ, so let the wives be to their own husbands in everything."

I could not memorize further; my mind was too agitated. "It just comes to this," I thought, "am I willing, for Christ's sake, to submit my will (in all but matters of conscience) to my husband?" The struggle was short but intense. At last I cried, *"For Christ's sake, I yield!"* Throwing a dressing gown about me, I ran to the top of the stairs and called to my friend, "When does the next train go?"

"In about half an hour," she replied, "but you couldn't catch it and have your breakfast."

"Never mind; I'm going to get that train!"

My friend insisted on accompanying me to the station; we ate as we almost ran. With what joy I at last found myself traveling northward!

On reaching my destination, imagine my surprise to find my husband, with a happy twinkle in his eye, standing on the platform!

"Why, Jonathan," I cried, "how did you know I was coming?"

His reply was simply a happy, "Oh, I knew you would come."

Later I told my husband frankly all that I had passed through. What was the result? From that time, he gave me my way as never before, for does not verse 25 of the chapter quoted go on to say: "Husbands, love your wives, even as Christ also loved the church, and gave himself for it." A new realization of the need of *yieldedness* came to us both and brought blessed results in our home life.

The Bible has always, since my conversion when a child of twelve, been a treasured companion. In the years when the children were small, with incessant calls upon me, I was unable, like my husband, to give hours a day to Bible study. I came to take the Bible as God's Word to me, often taking some promise for the day on which to lean. Sometimes, however, I dug into the Word with a concordance to find out what the Bible had to say on some matter on which at the time I needed help. I have before me as I write over forty outlines of such studies. Space permits but two of these.

We are told in the life of Frances Ridley Havergal by her sister that for many years, even after she had become known world-wide as a hymn writer, she was burdened with a sense of sin. I, too, for years, even after going to China, was often oppressed by the same burden of sin. One evening when all was quiet, I settled at my desk with Bible and concordance, determined to find out God's attitude toward the failures, the faults, and the sins of His children. The result of that study has been a blessing to myself and others:

What God Does with Our Sins

1. He lays them on His Son—Jesus Christ. Isa. 53:6
2. Christ takes them away. John 1:29
3. They are removed an immeasurable distance—as far as east is from west. Ps. 102:12
4. When sought for are not found. Jer. 50:20
5. The Lord forgives them. I John 1:9; Eph. 1:7; Ps. 103:3
6. He cleanses them ALL away by the blood of His Son. I John 1:7; Rev. 1:5
7. He cleanses them as white as snow or wool. Isa. 1:18; Ps. 51:7
8. He *abundantly* pardons them. Isa. 55:7
9. He tramples them under foot. Mic. 7:19 A.S.V.)
10. He remembers them no more. Heb. 10:17; Ezek. 33:16
11. He casts them behind His back. Isa. 38:17
12. He casts them into the *depths* of the sea. Mic. 7:19
13. He will not impute us with sins. Rom. 4:8
14. He covers them. Rom. 4:7
15. He blots them out. Isa. 43:25
16. He blots them out as a thick cloud. Isa. 44:22
17. He blots out even the proof against us, NAILING IT TO HIS SON'S CROSS. Col. 2:14

On one occasion, when giving this Bible study to a group of Christian Chinese women, when we came to "He remembers them no more," one woman rose and with a look of surprise and wonder, said, "Mrs. Goforth, do you really mean to say God forgets our sins when repented of?"

I replied, "The Bible says so, for 'He remembers them no more' means just that."

She remained standing silently for a moment, then exclaimed, "Then why should I torment myself about them? Oh, I'm so glad!"

It was while I had a large family of little children about me and mission work was pressing heavily upon me, while feeling burdened and that strength was insufficient, I sought to find in God's Word whether there were any conditions to be fulfilled for the receiving of divine strength. The result of this study was a surprise and joy to me, and later a blessing and help to many to whom I later passed it on, for *every condition the weakest could fulfill!*

Conditions of Receiving Strength
1. Weaknesses. II Cor. 12:9-10
2. No might. Isa. 40:29
3. Sitting still. Isa. 30:7
4. Waiting on God. Isa. 40:31
5. Quietness. Isa. 30:15
6. Confidence. Isa. 30:15
7. Joy in the Lord. Neh. 8:10
8. Poor. Isa. 25:4
9. Needy. Isa. 25:4
10. Abiding in Christ. Phil. 4:13 (A.S.V.)

I have been asked to write something on what I have reason to believe is the hardest problem of a foreign missionary mother's life. Perhaps in my case the problem—yes and the hardness—was extended over a longer period of time than most, as I had, as far as I know, the largest "foreign" family (with one exception) in the Far East— eleven children. The problem is that of separation either from husband or from children.

Much has been said on this subject, *especially by those in the homeland,* some going so far as to say missionaries should not have children. For many reasons it seems impossible to deal with this subject in a general way. All I can do is to try to give a glimpse of what this problem meant to me personally. I know my story could be duplicated in hundreds of other cases throughout the foreign field.

My husband was not a strong man physically. Early in his Knox College days he was threatened with a serious break in health through persistent indigestion. A Christian doctor, who took a special interest in him, wrote out a list of health rules he was to follow. In his characteristic way my husband, when possible, kept rigidly to these rules throughout his long life. I give this as it has an important bearing on the problem we are facing.

Those who have read *Goforth of China* will understand something of the exceedingly strenuous life my husband lived. Had he been left alone in China for years at a time to look after his own food, etc. when on his constant, long itineraries, I doubt whether he could long have survived such a test. It was this strong conviction that my husband needed me—that his very life depended on my care of him—that enabled me to bear the separation from the children as one by one they left the home nest for school, at first in China and then, as years passed, to cross the ocean for school in Canada.

The story I have been specially asked to give is the parting with my youngest—my baby. He was only six and a half years old. But it seemed to my husband good that he should be safe in the mission school at Weihuifu (our central station a few hours by train south of Changte). While we had no school near for our younger children, my husband felt we could look to the Lord to keep them safe when with us on the touring life, but not so when there was a school, etc. available. Oh, how I struggled to keep my child a little longer—he was so very young!

But at last the morning arrived when the child must be taken to Weihuifu. My husband, seeing how broken I was, tried to persuade me to allow him to take the little lad, but I was determined to keep him with me as long as possible. I kept calm outwardly until we arrived at the school. The children were all outside playing when we arrived. When my baby caught sight of them, he forgot me and dashed off to join in their fun.

It was necessary to leave again almost immediately in order to catch my return train, so after a few words with Miss S., Fred, my little boy, was sent for. I expected him to show some grief at parting, but the wee boy could scarcely spare time for a hasty hug and "Good-by, Mother, I want to play!"—and off he ran.

This unloosed the flood gates within me. I fled

weeping to my cart. Just as the cart was about to start, Mr. H. G. appeared, intending to accompany me to the station, but seeing what he did, he hastily returned home to inform Dr. L., who was going north by the same train, to look after me.

On reaching the station, I found a hiding place behind a big door. Try as I would, I could not stop my violent weeping. As the train drew into the station, I found a small seat behind the door, which permitted me to have my back to the other passengers in the car. Here I cried and sobbed. I felt like I imagined a lioness would feel who had been robbed of her whelps. Then as we neared our station of Changte, by desperate effort I calmed myself. When I glanced around, there was Dr. L. just behind me with a look of infinite pity, just waiting for a moment when he could speak. But his look of sympathy again opened the floodgates. Though a stranger and en route to Peking, he left the train at Changte and would not leave me till he had seen me safely home.

We had planned to leave on a long itinerary of our field as soon as possible after our wee boy had gone, but when I returned home to the empty house, for the first time in more than twenty years empty of children—my heart seemed as if it would break. For two days, instead of preparing for the coming journey, I lay and wept. My dear husband was tenderly sympathetic, but at last in desperation he became stern and insisted on my facing the future and turning my mind to the open door at hand. So, rising, I set to work and gradually this crisis in my life passed.

Turning from what has always been to me a

weepy story, I give the following which will strike a more cheerful note of this time.

Just before my little lad Fred and I reached Weihuifu, I said to him, "Now, Fred, I want you to try hard to be first in your class."

Months later, on reaching home for the holidays, he rushed in, in great excitement, shouting as he threw his arms about me, "Mother, I'm first; I'm first in my class."

When things had somewhat quieted down, I said, "And, Fred, how many have you in your class?"

His face fell as he replied, "Well, Mother, Miss S. put Alex Grant and me in a class by ourselves."

One of the most interesting experiences when I was with my husband on his distant tours was this:

Dr. Goforth had received an urgent call from Marshal Feng Yuhsiang to hold a revival mission among his soldiers. Later a telegram came asking me to accompany my husband for meetings among the officers' wives.

Never had I been more tested. A wave of intense wilting heat had gripped that part of China and was felt even on the mountaintop where the message reached us. What would it be on the plain below, where, we heard, cholera was raging! I was sorely tempted to listen to those who urged me not to go. Then, taking up my Bible with a cry for light, it opened to Ecclesiastes, the eleventh chapter. My eye resting on the fourth verse, which read: "He that observeth the wind shall not sow; and he that regardeth the cloud shall not reap."

How could I shrink back in the face of such words? Had I not gone, what I would have missed!

The heat was indeed intense and very trying, but, oh, the thrill that came from day to day when meeting with fifty or more officers' wives, most of whom were intelligent women of the higher class and could read. Many of the women's husbands were Christians, and eager that their wives, too, should be led to Christ. My last address was on the broad way and the narrow way. At the close, almost all indicated their wish to follow Christ.

One day the Marshal insisted on my addressing one thousand of his officers and men, telling the story of our escape from the Boxers in 1900. The meeting began with several hymns led by a choir and band. All started at once on the third stroke of the baton. No leading note was given. Every instrument in the band seemed to my ears to be turned to a different key. All played or sang as loudly as they could bang, toot, or shout. The effect was deafening and almost appalling. This had one good effect—driving away the excessive nervousness that had gripped me. When later, at a sign from the Marshal, I stepped forward and faced that great audience, calmness and power came to speak for over an hour on God's mighty miracle-working for us. And, oh, how they listened! The Marshal was right—it was indeed a message for Christian soldiers.

It was on this, our first visit to Marshal Feng's

camp, that my friendship with Mrs. Feng began and it continued to shortly before her death some years later, when we were home on a furlough. She died a true believer in the Lord.

One of the greatest—if not the greatest—and most far-reaching services in Dr. Goforth's life came through Marshal Feng and his army. It is to be hoped that some day the life of that truly great man may be given to the world by an unbiased writer. Through all the years, when later the Marshal undoubtedly had backslidden— even to many missionaries *hopelessly* so, Dr. Goforth never gave up hope for him, praying daily for his return. But it was not until some time after my husband's death that word began to come from various sources that revealed his prayers were being answered.

One missionary, who lived for some time as a neighbor of Marshal Feng and his family on Kuling Mountain, tells of his holding family worship each day and of his spending much time in daily Bible study. Another missionary recently told of the Marshal's passing through his station and addressing an overflow meeting. "He stressed the need of Christian truth in the heart if the individual or nation were to be saved. This truth, he declared, was to be found in the Bible, which he urged his hearers to read. The Marshal mentioned that several leading men in the government were feeling after Christ and were reading the Scriptures."

Chapter VII

HOW GOD TAUGHT ME
TO FORGIVE

*He that doth not forgive burns the bridge
over which he himself must needs pass, for
the Lord hath said, "If ye forgive not . . .
neither will your Father forgive your tres-
passes."* [1]

—*Selected*

THE TRAGIC STORY of how, but for the mercy
of God, that jagged rock of unforgiveness would
have wrecked me, body and soul, is given as a
solemn warning to others.

The first sad details of *how* and *why* the
demon of hate and unforgiveness entered my
heart cannot be given, for another is involved
who has passed on. Suffice it to say that those
who knew the facts agree that *humanly speaking*
one can scarcely imagine a case where unforgiveness was more justified. Yet my dear husband, who had equal reason with myself for feeling as I did, quietly and calmly laid it all before
the Lord and left it there and begged me to do

[1] Matt. 6:15.

88

the same, but I could not, or rather would not, forgive.

For more than a year, while the source of trouble remained at our station, I would not speak to or recognize that one. Four years passed, during which time the matter remained with me more or less in abeyance. Then one day my husband and I were traveling by train with a number of co-workers en route to the religious fair at Hsunhsein, where the most intensive and aggressive annual campaign of evangelism was carried on. This year I had been put in charge of the women's work there.

For months I had been deeply but secretly moved by the evident spiritual power that had come into my husband's life. I, his wife, could not but see that he was indeed filled with the Spirit of God. There had come into my soul a great yearning that I, too, might have this fullness of the Spirit.

As we sat there on the train that day, I asked my husband to sit with the others for I wanted to be alone. When he left, I bent my head and cried to God to fill me with His Spirit as He had filled my husband. Unmistakably clear came the Inner Voice, "Write to _____ (the one toward whom I felt hatred and unforgiveness), and ask forgiveness for the way you have treated him!" My whole soul cried out, "Never, never can I forgive him!" Again I prayed as before, and again the Inner Voice spoke clearly as before. Again I cried out in my heart, "Never, never. I will never forgive him!" When for the third time this was repeated, I jumped to my feet and said to myself, "I'll give it all up, for I'll never, never forgive!" I joined the others and laughed and talked to hide my agitation. Then followed the saddest part of my life. For several months I preached and prayed to keep up appearances, but all the while my heart was becoming harder, colder, and more hopeless.

Then one day that passage in the *Pilgrim's Progress* came to me (I think I was reading to the children), where Christian, going through the house of the Interpreter, came to the man in the cage who said, "I have grieved the Spirit, and He is gone; I have provoked God to anger, and He has left me." As I read this passage, a terrible conviction came upon me that the words I have quoted were true of me. During the two days and nights that followed, I was in the depths of despair, believing God's Holy Spirit had left me. My husband was away from home, and there seemed no one to whom I could turn. Then God in His mercy sent someone to me.

A young missionary, whose wife had died under peculiarly sad circumstances, was passing through our station and came over to see me. It was evening, and the children were in bed. We sat on the front steps together while he sobbingly told of his wife's tragic death. Suddenly the very floodgates seemed loosed within me, and I gave way to uncontrollable weeping. When able, I told all the story as I have related it, and its sad, early details; then I ended with, "I have grieved the Holy Spirit of God, and He has left me!"

"But Mrs. Goforth," he said, "are you willing to write the letter?"

I replied, "I now know what it would be to be without God and without hope, and if I could only have another chance, there is nothing I would not do."

Again he asked, "Are you willing to write that letter?"

"Yes," I replied.

"Then go at once and write it."

With a glorious ray of hope dawning in me, I ran into the house, and in a few minutes returned with the letter. It was just a few lines of humble apology for *my actions*, without any reference to the other part. Oh, the joy that came, and thankfulness that it was indeed not *too late!*

From that time, I have never DARED *not to forgive*. There have been times when for hours, or even days, the battle was on again, but always the remembrance of this experience has enabled me to conquer and forgive.

The following is one instance, which speaks for itself, of what this testimony has meant to others.

When addressing a large gathering of women in R—, an important town in Ontario, I felt strangely led to relate this story, though it had no connection with what went before or after. While the story was being told, a strange hush and marked stillness came over the audience. It was not till seven years later that I learned the reason for this. At the close of the annual meeting of the Women's Missionary Society in Ottawa, two women from the town of R— came up and told me the following striking story:

One of these women, Mrs. X., was the married daughter of a former pastor in R——. For years, while her father lived, she had led in the women's work of the church. When the new minister's wife, Mrs. S., attempted to take over the leadership of the women's work, trouble began. As time passed, a serious division arose, till at the time of my visit the whole church was divided. Practically all the women of both sides were present when I told the story of how the Lord taught me to forgive.

Mrs. S. went on to tell how, the morning I left, she had become so convicted and restless while preparing dinner she could stand it no longer. Leaving everything, she put on her hat and coat and started for the door, determined to go at once to Mrs. X. and make up. But before she reached the door, a knock came. On opening the door, she found Mrs. X. with outstretched hands and a look of love that could not be mistaken! On reaching this point of the story, Mrs. S. exclaimed, with a beaming face, "O Mrs. Goforth, it was so easy to make up, for she had been convicted just as I was. We have been the best of friends ever since."

It is Longfellow who wrote, "If we could only read the secret history of our enemies, we would find in each man's life sorrow and suffering enough to disarm all hostility." Is it not true that every time we repeat the Lord's Prayer with unforgiveness in our heart it is a challenge to the Father not to forgive? Otherwise, the words, "Forgive us as we forgive," have no meaning.

O God! that men would see a little clearer,
Or judge less harshly when we cannot see!
O God! that men would draw a little nearer
To one another. They'd be nearer Thee
      And UNDERSTOOD.

Chapter VIII

ANSWERED PRAYER
I

Prayer is the burden of a sigh,
  The falling of a tear,
The upward glancing of an eye,
  When none but God is near.
                    —Montgomery

How far from this conception of prayer is the too general thought of God's plan and purpose in providing a way of access to Himself! How hard prayer has been made by man-made rules! Oh, that we could catch a glimpse of the wonders, the power, and the *easiness*—yes, the *absolute necessity* of this God-planned provision, that it might have free course in our lives! Let us, dear fellow-climbers, learn to use God' wireless. The following is the most beautiful illustration of the simplicity of God's plan for the prayer life I have ever come across.

We were having a brief rest at Larges, Scotland, when a visitor told us the story, which I took down at the time: Near her lived a poor woman with a large family. Her husband was a laborer. They lived in a tiny house consisting of a "butt and ben." Unable to leave her family, the poor woman took in washing. A vivid picture was given of the woman, day by day at the tub or ironing board, with children and chickens about her. Then came the remarkable part of the story. The spiritual life of this woman was so deep and true that her influence for good was felt in a remarkable way throughout the whole region. Even the minister would often tether his horse by her door when passing and take a seat by her, as she went on with her work, for the inspiration and help she was to him.

One day he said, "My good friend, you always seem so near the Lord. How is it possible when you can never get alone with Him for quiet prayer?"

The woman, with a look of surprise, laid down her iron, seated herself, and said: "A, Meenister, that's whar ye mak' the mistake. Whan I wint tae shut a' oot I jist sit me doon in ma chair, an' throw ma apron owr ma heed, an' I'm in ma tabernacle alone wi' me Lord in a moment."

How beautiful, how wonderful to think that the secret of the overflowing spiritual power apprehended by that poor, hard-working, uneducated Scottish woman was the same that empowered and upheld the French mystic saint, Madam Guyon, who wrote:

> To me remains nor place nor time,
> My country is in every clime;
> I can be calm and free from care
> On any shore, since God is there.

Repeatedly people who have read the little book of testimonies to God's faithfulness in hearing and answering the cry of a mother when in need of help, have asked me the question: "Has God *continued* to answer?" (Many years have passed since the little book mentioned was written.) [1] The best answer to this, I believe, will be to give a few stories in which the facts speak for themselves. They are but a few, culled from many, all having taken place since the prayer testimonies referred to were published.

Financial Help in Time of Need

One winter, when in Toronto with the children (Mr. Goforth was in China), I was finding it very hard to make ends meet. About the middle of December, one of my sons came to me and said, "Mother, just look at this, my best suit. The pants are above the ankles, and look at my sleeves—inches above my wrists! I have just been made secretary of the _____ Club of the University. How can I face these men, many of them important leaders? I'm the worst dressed man in the University."

As I looked at the dear boy, I realized something of his humiliation at being forced to go about in such a suit, not only long outgrown but badly worn. I said, "My boy, there is no doubt it is a case of need. Let us stand on your father's great promise, 'My God shall supply all your need according to his riches in glory by Christ Jesus.' [2] I have not the money, but I be-

---

[1] *How I Know God Answers Prayer.*
[2] Phil. 4:19.

lieve God will give the money for a suit if we trust Him."

He started off to the University saying, "I wish I had your faith."

That day I went down to look for a suit, though I had no money to buy it. I found a beautiful, blue serge suit, but the price was fifty dollars. The words came, "According to his riches," and I said in my heart, "God is able to do this also." I returned home, of course without the suit, but sure that the money would come and I would be able to buy it.

The following day a letter came from a woman in far Wisconsin, U. S. A., whom I had met many years before at a convention. The letter enclosed a check for fifty dollars and read: "I am greatly interested in what you tell me of your children, particularly _____ [naming the boy needing the suit]. Please buy something for him with the enclosed fifty dollars!" How my heart thrilled at this evidence of the Lord's compassionate understanding! And my boy got his suit!

The following occurred some months after the incident just related. I had been six weeks in the Toronto General Hospital, during which time all mail had been brought to me by the children from home. One evening, a few days before I was to leave the hospital, my daughter came to me in evident distress. She said, "Mother, I hope you have plenty of money, for the bills have been mounting up terribly." When she left, I went over my accounts and found I had only twenty dollars to carry us over two weeks till the monthly check from the Board came. Several moments of intense worrying caused such faintness I became afraid. Putting the accounts away, I just committed all into the Lord's hands and fell asleep.

The following morning a letter lay on my breakfast tray. I expressed surprise to the nurse, and she said, "This letter came to the office last night as you were going to sleep, so we kept it till this morning." I found the letter to be from a close friend of my husband, Mr. R. H. It enclosed a check for one hundred dollars and read, "Please accept the enclosed as a personal gift. It may help a little in view of the near return of your husband." Truly at this moment the sense of the Lord's presence was very real. In acknowledging the gift, I wrote in part, "You have been just God's open channel; the gift is direct through you from my heavenly Father."

My failing sight was the chief reason for our return to Canada from Manchuria in 1930. I had become almost blind through cataracts in both eyes. Dr. Clarence Hill, of Toronto, operated on the left eye in July. The operation itself was an entire success. Some days later, when the eye was being dressed, the nurse failed to put a dark glass over the right eye, which for the first time was left uncovered. All through the bright, sunny day I used the eye constantly as visitor after visitor called. Then about sundown, I realized inflammation had set in. The inflammation increased so rapidly that by eight o'clock it had spread to the left eye. By eight-thirty the whole left side of my face had become inflamed and swollen. The pain was becoming unbearable.

Sharp pains were darting through the eye. I begged the supervisor to send for the doctor, but he was out of town. At last she agreed if I were no better by nine o'clock she would try to get help.

As she left, it came to me that the doctor could do nothing, as the mischief was already done. Then, in my distress I turned to the Lord with the conviction that He alone could meet the case. I confessed every sin and failure I could recall and promised obedience to God in all things. A great sense of peace came, though the distress and pain were getting more intense each moment. Then I cried, "O Lord, for blindness or sight, I put myself in Thy hands!" Instantly, as in a flash, all pain and swelling were gone! The cheek, which a moment before I dared not touch, I could and did rub as perfectly normal. Oh, the relief! I turned over and was nearly asleep when a young nurse came to inquire how I was. Sleepily, I said: "Tell the supervisor the Lord Jesus has touched my eye, and I'm all right."

When Dr. Hill later redressed the eye, he did not discover any sign of recent inflammation, nor did he learn of it till nine years later when I told him the experience.

We are told that in the mouth of two or three witnesses every word shall be established.

Witness No. I. Six weeks after the operation, Dr. Hill tested me for glasses. When asked to read the testing card, I read easily down to within two lines of the bottom. The doctor

Left: Jung da niang, the beloved Goforth amah who saved the life of Ruth in the Boxer Rebellion by letting the Boxers beat her almost to death rather than give up the child. *Below:* Goforth family picture taken in China about 1920. Paul and Helen were in Canada for their education. Back row, left to right, Ruth, Wallace and Mary. Front row left, to right, Jonathan Goforth, Fred, and Rosalind Goforth.

Above: Taken at Bei Tai He, the Goforth's summer home, around 1913. The children, from left to right are, Wallace, Mary, Fred, and Ruth. This was the house where Mary was born. By a miracle, she found it again when she visited China in 1980. *Left:* The Goforths used this sampan on a river that had many dangerous rapids, but they felt it was all supremely worthwhile because of the many converts at the end.

Below: Jonathan and Rosalind and a band of their trained helpers walking to an out-station for a day of preaching.

Above: After 1925, when the Goforths were invited back to their old Honan mission station for a three month tour, these fine, trained workers, converted under them, rallied around. The final tally was 3,000 converts. *Below:* Mrs. Su sai-guang, her husband, son and daughter. She is the daughter of Jonathan Goforth's most valued preacher-companion, Pastor Su, and is a preacher herself. The daughter, just graduated from university, has given her life to serve God, making three generations in His service. Mrs. Su is now a preacher in the Chang Chun Christian Church, which has grown phenomenally. At Christmas, 1982, the attendance was 900!

Pastor Su, a truly great Chinese gentleman. He and Jonathan Goforth were inseparable and devoted to each other and to their Master.

A Convention, in Shensi province, of Swedish missionaries. The Goforths were tremendously impressed by these people who had heart-rending stories to tell of their experiences during the Boxer Rebellion of 1900.

Above: Jonathan Goforth, now blind, with Rosalind, and Rev. and Mrs. T. B. Davis, and the Manchurian Band. In the last eight years of the Goforth ministry, forty-eight churches were established. *Left:* Jonathan Goforth and his daughter Helen's little Betty. The child's parents were Dr. and Mrs. George Van Gorder.

Right: Mary Goforth Moynan at six years of age. She is often referred to as "little Mary" in the Goforth books. Now she is carrying on the Goforth Ministries and promoting the books in many lands.

Above, left: Jonathan and Rosalind Goforth in China near the end of their ministry. *Above, right:* Jonathan and Rosalind, taken at Ben Lippen conference grounds, N. Carolina, in 1936, just a few days before he was taken home. They were the guests of Dr. and Mrs. Robert McQuilkin of the Columbia Bible College. *Below:* Jonathan and Rosalind Goforth taken at Keswick, N.J. by Mr. Herbert V. Hotchkiss of Los Angeles.

stopped me, saying, "Wonderful! The lower lines are for *abnormal* sight!"

Witness No. II. Nine months later Mr. Petrie, an old and well-known oculist, tested me for duplicate glasses in view of my leaving for China. When through with the testing, he turned to my husband and said, "Your wife has remarkable sight in that eye. I have been in the business for over thirty years and have never come across an eye that has been operated on for cataract that could see like hers."

Witness No. III. Two years later, feeling the need of freshening my reading glasses, I went with my husband to a young Chinese oculist in Dairen, Manchuria, who had been trained by a foreign doctor in Shanghai. When we came from the testing-room, this young man, in somewhat broken English, said to my husband, "She has velly good sight. She all same see like girl of twenty!"

Before writing this, I called on Dr. Clarence Hill to get his final—or rather, up-to-date—record regarding my sight. After careful examination, he said, "Your sight in that left eye has not failed in the slightest in these eight years."

A word further: during these eight years, my work has been almost constant eye strain. As my husband's secretary and secretary of the evangelistic fund—the latter requiring at one time the writing of six to eight hundred letters yearly—reading to my husband after he became blind, mission accounts, and later the writing of my husband's biography; through it all, I can recall having but one short period of slight inflammation in the operated eye, upon which I had wholly to depend!

Ah Lord, Jehovah! behold there is nothing
Too wonderful for thee.—Jer. 32:17 (A.S.V.)

We were stationed temporarily at Weihuifu, in the southern part of the Honan Field. When holding a women's study class at a distant outstation, I stayed in the home of Dr. Fan, the chief elder of the church there.

Just as the class was closing, Mrs. Fan asked me to visit a very sick boy, who had been sent home from the Weihuifu Mission Boys' School far gone with tuberculosis of the lungs. It was late afternoon when we reached the boy's home. We found the lad on a stool outside the door. My heart sank as I watched how he almost doubled up with every effort to get breath. Foam fell from his mouth, and his face had an ashen, deathly look. His mother and others gathered around as I prayed. But it seemed hypocrisy for me to pray that he might be healed, for I simply had not the faith for such a miracle. So I prayed for the mother and finally ended by praying that the boy might be given *dying grace!*

Then, as we started back across the fields, these words kept ringing in my ears, "Call for the elders of the church; and let them pray over him." [3] Over and over again these words came, till on reaching the Fans' home I determined just to obey, though I could not work up any faith that the boy would live. I would *blindly obey.*

---

[3] James 5:14.

But when I told Dr. Fan what I wanted to do, he at first refused to join me, saying, "Why, the boy is dying!" But I persisted, and he gave way as I said, "Dr. Fan, I honestly have not the faith to believe for the boy's healing, but if I return home without at least obeying what seems like God's voice, I will be utterly miserable and conscience-stricken."

The boy was brought. Elders and friends gathered about, and the boy was placed in the midst. We all knelt on the earthen floor. The elders prayed. Then I closed, praying much as I had before. The boy was taken home, and the following morning I left for Changte.

A year later, when attending presbytery at Weihuifu, I met Mrs. Fan and inquired, *"Did that boy die?"* (Oh, the sadness of no faith!)

The reply came, "Why, no, the lad is quite well and helping his father!"

Two years passed, and I was again at Weihuifu helping Miss McI. with special meetings for women. One day, as we sat at dinner and I was telling her this story, a knock came on the door, and in walked a tall, strong, fine-looking young man, the photographer who had taken several pictures for us the previous day. He handed Miss McI. the photos with a few words; then, turning to me, he said (of course in Chinese), "I see you do not know me, Mrs. Goforth."

I replied, "No, I have no remembrance of having seen you before."

At this he smiled and, coming forward, gave me a bow, saying, "I am the boy you prayed for almost three years ago. I have never forgotten you."

Words could never describe my feelings at this moment. Glad, yes, but oh, so sad and humbled! Then came a glimpse of God's infinite love and patience in using such a faithless channel to work His miracle. Truly as the heavens are high above the earth, so are His ways higher than our ways! [4]

The Great War was over. Word had reached us in China of our son, who had given several years' service, now being at "loose ends." My heart longed for my boy with such passionate longing I went to my husband and begged him to let me go to him, for I believed the boy needed me in what seemed a crisis in his life. But my husband made it quite plain finances alone would make it impossible for me to take the journey to Canada.

The burden, the longing for the child, continued. I determined to say no more but just pray. I began at last to pray definitely that if I could not go to my boy he might find some way of coming to us.

We were on the Kuling mountain a few weeks later, in July, holding meetings for missionaries. One Sunday evening while at supper a special delivery letter was handed to me. It had a Japanese stamp and was addressed in my son's handwriting. My heart seemed to stand still as I whispered to my husband, "Our boy is in Japan."

---

[4] Isa. 55:8, 9.

The letter stated he was working his way across the Pacific on a freighter and would be in a Manchurian port only a week before returning to Canada. He ended by saying, "Mother, make for Newchwang as quickly as possible. You may reach there before I do."

A chapter could well be given to that long journey of well nigh two thousand miles in the intense heat of midsummer and to the unique experience of arriving in the strange city of Newchwang in a drenching rain. I could but follow the crowd in semidarkness from railway station to ferry. When I reached the Newchwang side of the river, darkness had set in. With great difficulty two *rickshas* were secured and directed to the office of the steamship company. But when I arrived there, all was in darkness and locked up. I then ordered the *ricksha* men to take me to the one good hotel.

As I alighted from my *ricksha* and was about to enter the hotel door, a flood of water came pouring down from the roof, drenching me from head to foot. In this condition, I entered the lobby and faced an immaculate Chinese hotel "boy" (waiter). In response to my request for a room came the answer, with a provoking smile of amusement, "Velly solly, Missis. No room, can have place two days come!"

The *ricksha* man, who had followed me in, stepped forward, and said, "You come with me, Missis; I take you Mission."

I hesitated, for it was risky, but the man had a kind look. So, committing myself to the Lord, I went once more out into darkness, drenching rain, and slush. After what seemed an endless ride, the mission gate was reached about ten o'clock.

After several minutes' pounding on the gate, it opened a few inches; but the gatekeeper utterly refused to admit us, saying the missionaries were away. I had put my foot in just far enough so the door could not close. An inspiration born of desperation came to me. I said, "Old gentleman, were you here when Dr. Goforth led the revival meetings?"

"Yes, I was," came the answer.

"Then you will let me in. I am Mrs. Goforth."

At once the door flew wide open!

Then followed one of the strangest experiences of my life. The gatekeeper led me into the house, which I literally took by storm. First I was shown into a bedroom, evidently made ready for someone, for even the bedclothes were turned back. When told this was "for Master, expected at midnight," I fled. In the next room, the bedstead had been taken down. There was no time to lose, for I was shivering in my wet clothes, so we set to and managed at last to get the heavy, very large iron bedstead set up. Mattresses had evidently been put in the storeroom for summer, for none could be found. At last, locking the door, I spread what dry clothes I had on the bed springs and slept soundly till nine o'clock the following morning. When I realized what I had done, I dreaded facing the strange master of the house. I stood fearfully several minutes before summoning up courage to open the door. When I did so, I found the "Master" in the hall await-

ing my appearance and looking as scared as I
felt, but only for a moment. Then came, "Why,
Mrs. Goforth!" My host, with evident relief, then
told of meeting Dr. Goforth and myself at a
convention in Moyallon, Ireland in 1910.

My troubles were over. Every possible kindness and courtesy was extended to me and to
my son, who arrived the following day. Our
host then left us for his holiday at Peitaiho, giving us the full run of his house and a servant
to attend us.

How fully God answered prayer!

When the separation time came a week later,
my boy left me with new hope and courage for
the future.

My train left an hour or two before his boat
sailed. Try to imagine my feeling when, just as
the train began to move, my boy came racing
across the platform and thrust into my hand a
small parcel, saying, "Mother, dear, it is all I
have. The steward says you'll enjoy it, for it's
the best *Canadian butter!*"

I turned with my pound of "best Canadian
butter" to force my way into a packed car with
the thermometer well up to the one hundred
mark. The only place for the butter was my
hand bag. After placing it there, intending to
throw it out of the window, if necessary, I
promptly forgot it. Many hours later, when I
reached my destination at midnight, toilet articles and other things were found to be soaking
in a bed of butter oil!

We were on furlough. Spring had come in with

sudden warmth. A great heap of children's clothes lay before me, each needing some attention, some alteration to keep pace with the growing children. A burden of worry seized me. Turning to my husband nearby, deep, as usual, in his beloved Bible, I cried: "Jonathan, I simply must cancel my speaking engagements. It is utterly impossible for me to do all this sewing and take meetings, too."

He replied, "My dear, you will do no such thing. God has given you a message to deliver, and you must deliver it. Just go downtown and buy some ready-made garments."

"But," I replied, "think of the money that would cost. We cannot afford it."

Quietly came the answer, "Then trust the Lord to send the money!" Feeling the hopelessness of making him understand, I went into the adjoining room and, sinking on my knees, cried out my need. Then there came the conviction that my husband was right. Rising, I determined to trust and not worry.

The following afternoon I addressed a presbyterial gathering in western Ontario. The meeting closed too late to catch the train back to Toronto. That evening Dr. R. P. McKay, our foreign-mission secretary, addressed a packed church. An elderly man and myself occupied seats immediately in front of the pulpit. He evidently took a deep interest in the address, judging by his all too audible and frequent *amens*. Turning to me, he whispered, "Did you hear Mrs. Goforth this afternoon?"

"Yes," I replied with a sign for him to be quiet.

"Wasn't she————" he began, but I interrupted, fearing he might say something I should not hear.

"I am Mrs. Goforth," I said, with which he seemed quite to forget where he was. Grasping both my hands with great delight, he began to talk as if we were alone. I whispered back to him to be still, as we were disturbing the meeting. For a brief spell, he did keep still. Then, as I watched out of the corner of my eye, to my horror I saw him take out his purse with the evident intention of giving me money before the eyes watching us from the gallery. This was too much. In a panic, I sought for some way to escape. At that very instant, Dr. McKay gave out a hymn, saying all who needed to catch the local train could leave. With a sense of utter relief, I took advantage of this and went to a seat by the door. At the close of the meeting, many shook hands when passing out, among them my elderly man. On reaching me, he pressed into my hand some money in bills. As he bent forward, he whispered, "This is for your children. They must need things!" Oh, the wonder of it! But it was not simply the answer to prayer that made it difficult to hide my emotion; even more, the simple, kind, understanding look with which it was given.

On reaching my room I was amazed at the amount of the gift. I need not describe the scene when, on reaching Toronto, I related all to my husband. I felt very, very humbled, and well do

I remember the happy, shining look of victory in his face as he said, "Yes, dear, it is but one more proof of God's faithfulness."

The above would not be complete without the following:

My husband and I were to speak at S—, an important center in Ontario. On arriving at the station, we were met by the minister and, to my great surprise and delight, my elderly man of the presbyterial meeting, Mr. S—. My husband walked with the minister, while a place was made for me in a buggy beside Mr. S—. We had not gone far when the old saint turned to me with tears in his eyes and said, "Mrs. Goforth, I would give all I have, *anything* if I could know certainly that I am really born again. I feel so unworthy of being a child of God."

We talked for a few brief moments, while I prayed in my heart for wisdom. Then I said, "Dear friend, do you love God's children?"

"Oh, yes," he answered, "I love anyone and everyone whom I know loves the Lord."

"Then," I said, "I *know* you are born again, for John, the Lord's beloved disciple, said, *We know that we have passed out of death into life, because we love the brethren.*" [5] A few moments of silence passed. Then dear Mr. S.— turned to me with a bright smile, saying, "I never realized the truth of that word before."

Soon after reaching China, sometime later, word came of this saint having passed through the veil. Some day I expect to see him again and

---

[5] I John 3:14 (A. S. V.).

have time then to tell him of all the wonderful
things bought with God's gift sent through him,
His humble channel.

Chapter IX

ANSWERED PRAYER
II

What would happen if we all believed God?

As I write of answered prayer, there comes the remembrance of so many occasions when prayer was answered in connection with the addressing of meetings that I simply cannot attempt to record them all. I shall give just two stories to illustrate how definitely the Lord helped, at such times, in direct answer to prayer.

The first of these occurred when we were on furlough. I had four small children. My husband was away when one of the children became seriously ill. I was due to address the presbyterial meeting in Chalmers Church, Toronto. I was up with my sick child the night previous to this meeting and was pressed to the utmost right up to the time I had to leave for the meeting. I was so worn out and sleepy I actually fell asleep in the streetcar, and when I was on the platform, waiting my turn to speak, my head kept nodding. Try as I would, I could not get my brain to work and was utterly at a loss as to what to say. The church was packed. As I rose to address that great audience, I seemed to feel the Lord beside me. My mind then cleared, and for an hour the audience listened with great stillness. The Lord had heard my desperate cry and had given calmness and power. No one, I believe, knew what that meeting meant to me. He had, as often before and since, just *brought me through!* [1]

The second incident that now comes to mind occurred in our station of Changte, North Honan. We missionary wives, including Dr. Jean Dow, were supposed to take turns in leading the Chinese women's Wednesday afternoon prayer meeting. Sometimes a note would come from a fellow-worker well after two o'clock, (the meeting began at three o'clock) asking me to take the meeting for her.

One afternoon, when I was especially busy, such a note reached me. What could I do? There was the baby to nurse, and some message must be thought out. Hastily taking up the baby, I opened the Bible and placed it on a chair near enough to see, but at a safe distance from little, grasping hands. (Every mother knows a baby fights against divided attention!) Just then my husband opened the door. He exclaimed, "Well, Rose! It puzzles me how you can address a meeting with so little preparation."

I replied: "Jonathan, if I had time like you, I could not expect to get a message in so short a time, but the fact is the Lord suits His help to me as a mother!" And, oh, so often He did.

---

[1] See Ezek. 47:3, 4.

(That afternoon the Lord gave a blessed message.)

I remember how when home in 1910 I addressed, during that furlough over two hundred and fifty meetings. I had five children to care for then, and many times it was not till I was dressing to go to the meeting that, as I cast myself down on my knees for a moment, there came to me the clear-cut outline of the message I was to give. It was wonderful! It was D. L. Moody who once said, "The Christian on his knees sees more than the philosopher on tiptoe."

Sadly and humbly, I must confess that many, many times when I had cried to the Lord for power in speaking and evident power was given, I had not left the platform before the thought would come, "*I* have done well today." Then would come the cry for forgiveness.

In my little book of prayer testimonies, *How I Know God Answers Prayer,* a chapter is given to the Lord's gracious answers to prayer on the 1910-11 furlough.

The definiteness of the divine leading in connection with the great famine of 1920-21 was remarkable. We give the story to the "praise of the glory of His grace," through which alone the work was attempted and accomplished.

I was unable, because of illness, to accompany my husband as he left our home on Kikungshan Mountain in the late summer of 1920. The news of the great famine reached me there in a letter from a co-worker in Changte. The letter described vividly some of the awful conditions prevailing throughout our whole field, which was in the center of a vast area affecting, it was said, from thirty to forty millions of people. The picture given of what the writer himself saw was heartrending.

Crushed at the thought of what hundreds of those who looked upon us as mother and father were passing through, I cried aloud in agony of soul, "O God, is there not something I can do? Oh, show me!"

Clearly came the answer, "Use your pen!"

Hastening to my desk, I prayed as I prepared to write, "Lord, use my pen!" Just one sheet was written, giving briefly the facts Mr. X. had given in his letter. At once this was taken to a neighbor who had a mimeograph. One hundred and fifty copies were quickly turned off, and these were distributed among the various nationalities —about ten in all—then on the mountain. Within twenty-four hours of the writing of the appeal it was translated into several languages and on its way throughout the world!

Realizing that some donations might come to me, I took steps at once to get official permission for receiving and disbursing famine funds. Chapters could be written on the months that followed, but space permits of but a few facts. Before the famine of 1920-21 ended, I had received over one hundred and twenty thousand dollars for famine relief. I kept closely in touch with several relief centers, and to these I sent checks as needed. Many were the thrills that came that winter as appeals reached me, and I was able to write checks off the Famine Relief

Fund for amounts of $5,000 or even $10,000.

One incident may be given as indicative of many others. While waiting for the train at an important junction (we were visiting relief centers), two missionaries came up to us. One was leaving on our train; the other resided at the junction. Of the latter I inquired, "How about the relief work here?"

He replied, "All soup kitchens will have to be closed tomorrow, as our funds are exhausted, and it will be ten days before more funds can reach us."

"How much money would be sufficient to carry on for these ten days?" I asked.

"Five hundred dollars," was the answer. Signing for him to follow me, I led to where my satchel lay in the waiting room. Opening my Famine Relief checkbook, a check for five hundred dollars was quickly made out and handed to the missionary, who fairly gasped, "But you can't afford this much!"

Joyously I answered, "No, but though poor, I am making many rich!" Our train was in sight, so there was only time to tell briefly the story given.

As the famine was ending, the chairman of an important relief center stated publicly that "no one could ever tell how many hundreds of thousands of dollars had come in to the various relief centers as a result of Mrs. Goforth's timely appeal, nor how many lives had thus been saved." On hearing this, I could but bow my head in wonder and praise, for truly it had been the

Lord's doing. All I had done was to receive and acknowledge the donations and forward the money to relief workers.

Hudson Taylor once said, "How often do we attempt work for God to the limit of our incompetency rather than to the limit of God's omnipotency." The famine relief experience, as I recalled it, always seemed to me the one time in my life when I had attempted and carried out a ministry "to the limit of God's omnipotency."

The following should be recorded here as an outcome, or sequel, of the famine ministry.

The autumn following the great famine found us starting on a long campaign of tent evangelism for the whole of Changte field. Not a few details of that wonderful tour are given in *Goforth of China*.[2] What I wish to record here briefly is something of what that winter meant to me personally. Little did I dream that it was to be my last, long itinerary in our old Changte field.

The weather was becoming very cold when we started off. Practically every place at which we stayed had paper windows, with many openings through which wind and rain could enter The meetings were held in drafty, impromptu made mat tents or sheds through which the bit ter wind swept mercilessly. No place was heated. But, oh, the experience was wonderful to me, especially during the first months while I was able to enter into and take part in the campaign. Everywhere hearts were opened to the Gospel message as a result of the splendidly organized famine relief carried on all through the previous

---

[2] *Goforth of China*, chapter XIX.

winter by the band of faithful missionaries in Changte, often at the risk of their lives.

As the weeks passed, the increasingly bitter cold, the constant strain, the general hardness of the tour, began to tell on me. My dear husband, who never spared himself, never complained and was a wonderful, living example of love, patience, and fortitude that won all to himself and to his Saviour.

After about two months touring the hilly region to the west, we returned to Changte for presbytery in December, again starting off in January, this time to reach the main centers of the eastern section of the field.

While at Takwanchwang, the first place of our "tour," I caught a severe cold on my chest. The question was, Should I give up the trip and return to Changte? To do so would largely break up the women's part of the campaign. So I decided just to go on and pray for strength at least to play the organ and conduct the singing in the tent. Later it almost seemed I should have gone back, for, as we traveled southward a day's journey, I became worse with what seemed pleurisy. Our home at this second place was a damp, mud hut.

To go from place to place on that journey, where every moment was a prayer for help, would weary the reader. Sometimes, though very seldom, we found ourselves in a comparatively comfortable, heated room. Sometimes I was able to take part in the preaching to crowds of women, who literally clamored for the foreign woman to address them.

At last we started for the farthest, most northern point of the field. The day was stormy, cold, and rainy. How I prayed that we might get to a *warm* place, but alas, we were shown into a large, barn-like room! The paper windows had many holes, through which the wind and rain swept. Later these windows were papered over, but many holes in the roof remained.

As I recall the days spent in that room, it all seems one of the darkest, hardest physical experiences of my life. I had again caught a severe chill and was feverish and in pain. I forced myself to attend the first few meetings but finally had to give in. I tried to get warm with a hot water bottle and everything my husband could pile on me on the brick bed. But it was no use. I simply got colder and colder. As my husband left for the meeting, I rose and began to pace the rough, earthen floor, crying aloud in agony, "O Lord, have You no pity? Oh, help me! Why should I suffer so?"

Just then the two-leaf door was flung open and a coolie entered. On his shoulder was balanced a bamboo pole with a fully laden basket on each end. He handed me a letter. It was from some American missionaries living quite a distance from where we were. These missionaries had spent a few hours with us the day before to see something of my husband's methods of work. They had stayed for dinner and had left us with practically an empty larder. They must have sensed this, as the two laden baskets indicated. These contained all sorts of good things—jam, pickles, bread, cake, butter, and other things.

But the most timely and precious evidence of God's love and care came, when tearing paper off a bottle of grape juice, I noticed a portion of the torn paper lying on the floor on which, in large print, were the words,

"IS THIS THE RIGHT ROAD HOME?"

Picking up the bit of paper, I read the following lines:

Is THIS the right road home, O Lord?
The clouds are dark and still,
The stony path is sharp and hard,
Each step brings some fresh hill!
I thought the way would brighter grow
And that the sun with warmth would glow
And joyous songs from free hearts flow.
    Is THIS the right road home?

Yes, child! this very path I trod,
The clouds were dark for Me,
The stony path was hard to tread,
Not sight but faith can see
That at the end the sun shines bright,
Forever where there is no night,
And glad hearts rest from earth's fierce fight,
    It IS the right road home!

On carefully examining the scrap of paper, I found it to be a portion of an English paper, "The Life of Faith," printed four years before in 1914 at the time of the Great War. How strange! How wonderful! God surely, in this case, moved in a mysterious way. An English newspaper four years old, coming through American missionaries and reaching me, as it did, just when I needed the message desperately!

Again and again I read those lines, which seemed to speak to me a message from the Lord direct to my soul. At last I cried out, "O Lord, if this I am now going through is the right road home, then I will not murmur!"

Two days later, our way took us near the railway. Leaving the others to continue the remaining ten days of the tour, I returned to Changte. Miss McI— opened the door of the single women's home in response to my knock. As she looked at me, she fairly gasped, "It surely is not Mrs. Goforth!" Later she told me I looked simply a ghost of myself.

Oh, the blessedness of the week that followed! All three women, Miss McI—, Dr. D—, and Miss P—, vied with each other in caring for me as I lay at last in a warm, clean, lovely bedroom.

The effects of what I had gone through those months remained with me for years. But *He brought me through!* And so will He do for you, dear fellow-climber.

The following two incidents illustrate the truth of the words:

> Prayer is the soul's sincere desire,
> Uttered or unexpressed.

My husband and I were in New York holding meetings. I was writing a brief story of Miss Cornelia Bonnell, "The Angel of Shanghai." [3] One morning as we sat together in our room, I was finishing the story as far as I could go,

---

[3] *Miracle Lives of China*, chap. XIII.

but it was entirely lacking in any reference to her early life, as I had failed to contact anyone who could give me any data of that period. At last I laid down my pen and said to my husband, "Oh, how I wish I could find someone who knew Miss Bonnell in those early years and could give me what I need to finish this story!"

A few moments later, I started for the office downstairs for some stamps. As I entered the small elevator, I said to the elevator girl (quite a stranger to me), "I am writing the story of a wonderful missionary, but I don't know anything of her early life, and the sketch will be incomplete as it is."

The girl asked: "Who is it you are writing about?"

I replied: "Miss Cornelia Bonnell, of the Door of Hope, Shanghai."

The girl exclaimed: "Why, Mrs. Goforth, how strange! I have known Cornelia Bonnell and her family since we were girls together at school. I can give you all the facts you want."

This she did a few hours later, and before we left New York, the sketch was finished.

The second incident along this line occurred in inland China as we were traveling by train to a certain station.

I had my writing pad on my lap and was writing the sketch, "From Servant to Superintendent," [4] the story of Yang Yu-ming, one of our early schoolboys who had "made good." I was entirely familiar with his life up to the time he

---

[4] *Miracle Lives of China,* chap. V.

was sent by the Chinese postal authorities on a long and hazardous journey to the province of Sinkiang. It was a pioneer mission of the utmost importance—the opening up of post offices in the farthest northwest of China. We lost sight of him after he left on this mission until, many months later, word came of his death. I was nearing the end of the story and wished greatly I could know something of Yang Yu-ming's life in that far distant region.

Just then a China Inland missionary came aboard, a stranger to us. As he and my husband talked together, I excused myself, saying: "I am writing the story of Yang Yu-ming, one of our early schoolboys."

With a look of surprise, the missionary said: "How strange! Not the Mr. Yang who came to my station in Sinkiang?"

Then he told of his being the only missionary in that far distant province and how Yang Yu-ming had made his headquarters in the same city near his mission and had lived there till the time of his death. As he talked just the facts I had been wanting were given—and what a story it was of Yang Yu-ming's loving, faithful service for his divine Master, whom he served with the utmost faithfulness (and also human masters) even unto death.

I never had a shadow of doubt that God led that missionary to our train. He was the *only one* who could have given me the personal touches and facts I needed. Some may say, "Just a coincidence," but I would rather trace God's hand in it all.

More than once in my life have I experienced the blessing and reward that come as a result of obedience to what seems to be the Inner Voice.

The following two stories illustrate the importance of obedience to this prompting and also the tragic consequences of disobedience:

One morning (in Toronto) I was busy sewing, in view of an early return to China. The thought of two dear friends of the China Inland Mission kept coming persistently. They were also on furlough. At last I thought, "Perhaps this means that I should send them a gift." Looking into my purse, I found I had less than a dollar to do till my husband returned the following morning. Just then the mail came with a letter from a distant country village where I had spoken when visiting a friend more than *a year before,* not, of course, expecting to receive money. The letter enclosed five dollars and said, "By some mistake this was not sent you before." At once I decided this so unexpected gift should be sent Miss L. and Mrs. T., but waited till my husband returned. He gladly added ten dollars to my five, which was sent off at once to my friends.

Three days later came a letter from Mrs. T. saying she and Miss L. had for some days been praying for money to meet a certain need. The morning my letter reached them they had said to one another, "Assuredly this need will be met." The morning mail brought my letter, and the afternoon mail brought a letter from another friend, also enclosing a gift. The two amounts came to just the sum required to meet their need.

But, oh, the tragedy of not obeying! A dear

friend had gone to England on a visit. When word of this reached me in central China, there came a distinct urge to write to a family friend in England, Mr. B., giving him her address. Each time this urge came to me, I said: "Yes, yes, I will write to him. But I'm too busy just now." This lasted a whole month, and the letter was never written, for the urge ceased and the matter was forgotten. Six years later, on returning to Canada, I learned that Mr. B. had written his home people in Canada in vain, asking for my friend's address. It seemed the two had had a difference that had brought about a separation. Mr. B. hoped for a reconciliation if he could see her. My friend was wondering in the meantime why he did not come. Had I but obeyed the definite urge—I believe, of the Holy Spirit—all would have been well. But my friend returned to Canada without their meeting, and three years later Mr. B. died.

Quite recently I felt urged to visit an old bed-ridden woman who, I was told, wished to see me, but again I put off going. Then word came of her sudden passing! How sorry I was, but too late!

And as thy servant was busy here and there, he was gone (I Kings 20:40).

Early in 1923 my health was such that I was forced to return to our home on Kikungshan Mountain, leaving my husband to continue a marvelous ministry then progressing in Marshal Feng's camp near Peking.

Unfit, at least temporarily, for active mission work, I began to pray the Lord to undertake for me in providing the funds, if it was His will that I should go to my children in Canada. I had written to a friend in Hongkong telling of my circumstances and my wish to return to Canada.

A few weeks later, I received a letter from this friend. She wrote of how the night following the arrival of my letter she could not sleep, and she gave herself to praying for me. She asked the Lord to show her if there was anything she could do. The impression came strongly to write to a friend of her husband who had influence in the Canadian Pacific at Hongkong. This she did the following morning. A few hours later came the answer to the effect that word had been sent to the Shanghai office to honor my order up to $1,000. My friend closed with: "A first-class cabin and passage have been secured and instruc-' tions given that you are to receive special attention. So all you have to do is *float gently home!*"

When in the homeland we sometimes told stories that our good Christian, but skeptical, home people would not believe. Here is one:

One of my Bible women, Mrs. Li, had a little grandchild whose right arm had become paralyzed. The father was a doctor trained by our Dr. Leslie. Everything had been done for the child, but the arm remained limp and useless.

Mrs. Li had accompanied us to Linching for a week's revival meetings among the Christians. One morning when a wonderful spiritual movement was on, Mrs. Li became deeply convicted of certain things in her life. Humbly and quietly, not aloud, she confessed all to the Lord. Then there came the remembrance of her beloved grandchild's condition. She pleaded earnestly that the Lord might heal the child. A few days later, at the close of the meetings, Mrs. Li returned home and was welcomed by her daughter-in-law holding the child, *both* of whose arms were outstretched! On inquiring when the healing came, Mrs. Li found it was at the time of the revival-meeting, while she prayed.

Behold, I am the Lord, the God of all flesh: is there anything too hard for me? (Jer. 32:27).

Chapter X

FURLOUGH MEMORIES

He goeth before—

THE SUMMER of 1908 found me with five children again facing a long journey, this time homeward, Dr. Goforth remaining in China for the revival missions opening to him on all sides.

In some unaccountable way, on our arrival at Vancouver, no one met us, so we went at once to the nearest hotel, reaching there about 8:00 A.M. The hotel register signed, we were marched off to a *small* elevator, or "lift," as it was called. When all were in, we were pretty closely packed. Just before the start upward began, W. W., in a deep stage whisper, said, "Well, Mother, I think they are giving us a *pretty small bedroom!*" (I had warned the children that the bedrooms would be small.) The elevator boy seemed so overcome by the remark that it was some moments before he could start upward. Reaching our floor, we filed out into a large, square hall, where a maid was using a carpet sweeper. Again the irrepressible W. W., in his far-reaching whisper, exclaimed, with a look of surprise, "O Mother,

look at that woman; she is sweeping the carpet
with a lawn mower!"

We had arrived in Vancouver on Saturday.
I found I would need someone to identify me
before my draft could be cashed. I hunted up
in the telephone book the name and address of
a Presbyterian minister, who, I felt sure, would
know of Dr. Goforth and help me.

I started off that boiling hot Saturday and
never can I forget the sense of utter bewilder-
ment and loneliness that came over me—a
stranger in a strange land! Twice I lost my way.
At last the right street was found, but after walking what seemed an endless distance, I ventured
to ask at a door how far it was to the Rev.
Blank's home.

The woman I addressed looked at me pity-
ingly and replied, "You poor dear; you look just
dead beat. Come in, I'll get you some tea in a
jiffy!"

Since a "cup of cold water" will receive its
reward, that woman must long ere this have received a reward for that cup of tea! Rested,
strengthened, and cheered by her kindness, I
went on my way. But she really had looked at
me as if I were a *female tramp!* No doubt I did
look queer, for on reaching Dr. Blank's home,
the maid left me standing in the hall while she
carried my message to her master. Returning,
she coldly signed for me to take the hall chair.
After I waited a long time, Dr. Blank appeared.
I rose and told briefly my story, he, the while,
eying me suspiciously. I was then invited into
the study, where he plied me with many ques-

tions, all indicating his determination to make quite sure *I was not a fraud*. Then suddenly he looked at his watch and rose, saying, "We have just time to reach the bank before closing."

On reaching the bank, this gentleman introduced me to the teller and when assured all was right, raised his hat courteously and disappeared. A lump came in my throat as I sought to find my way back to the hotel.

That afternoon my oldest daughter, seeing I was feeling rather down, suggested leaving the children with Ruth and taking a walk.

We were undoubtedly unsophisticated in matters of fashion, coming as we did fresh from the heart of China. What we saw on that crowded street almost took our breath away. "Merry Widow" hats were in vogue. I could hear Helen gasp, "Oh, oh," as some especially striking head adornment drew near. I expected every moment to hear her ask me to buy some such thing for her; I was therefore indeed amazed when she turned to me with, "Mother, dear, isn't it simply awful? *Can't we go back to China on the boat we came by?*"

Just as we reached our hotel, we came face to face with the Rev. H. G., of Honan, an honored friend and co-worker. He was to sail for China with his wife and family on the same boat on which we had come. This good man, though pressed with many matters of his own, simply took charge of us all, to my unbounded relief.

A little incident illustrating not physical or spiritual but *inner* blindness occurred when passing through the most wonderful part of the Rocky Mountain region. The day was perfect, with just enough fleecy clouds to enhance the grandeur and gorgeousness of the snow-capped peaks. Even the younger children were thrilled with the wonderful scenery through which we were passing. Helen was constantly signing to me to share with her some specially exquisite scene.

On the car with us were a husband and wife with their twelve-year-old daughter. They were workers in Japan, and we had crossed the Pacific together. To my amazement, while passing through the most beautiful scenery, these good people drew down their blind and played flinch. Thinking they had not noticed the outside view, I ventured over to them and said, "The scenery is simply marvelous," but the blank, cold stare with which this remark was greeted sent me back to my seat, wondering how it could be possible that human beings, and "refined" ones, could be so absolutely *blind*.

On reaching one of the larger places en route, just as the children were being settled in their berths for the night, someone drew aside the curtain, saying, "There are ice cream cones being sold here." As "cones" had come in since my last furlough, I really did not know what the word meant, but "ice cream" was sufficiently attractive. So I said, "Get enough for all of us."

How I wish it were possible to have taken a "snap" of the children as their first cones were handled and enjoyed. Silence reigned for a brief spell; then one child cried out mournfully, "Say,

Mother, I can't get at all my ice cream. My tongue won't reach down far enough!"

I called to a fellow passenger, "How ever can the children get all the ice cream?"

With a hearty laugh, the reply came, "Why, eat the cone, of course."

I may say just here the following incidents are not given in the order in which they occurred, but as memory brings them to mind.

The following incident occurred in old St. John's Presbyterian Church, Toronto. The building had been enlarged from a mission hall. The minister, the Rev. J. McP. Scott, was our friend of many years.

One Sunday morning, when seated well back in the church, I was startled to hear Dr. Scott announce, "We will sing hymn number——. Then will Mrs. Goforth please come forward and at the close of the hymn lead us in the Lord's prayer in Chinese." I knew the prayer in Chinese quite as well as I did in English, but the suddenness of the call left my mind absolutely blank. If I could only have recalled the first Chinese word, I could have gone on, but I could not. While they were singing the hymn, I walked forward slowly, saying to myself in an agony of desperation: "How does it begin? How does it begin?" The platform was reached, and stepping forward to where Dr. Scott pointed, I found the congregation were already waiting with heads bowed. What could I do? Then there flashed into my mind the hymn, "Jesus Loves Me," in Chinese. Without a tremor, I repeated slowly the first two verses with the chorus, *about the length of the Lord's prayer*. Then all the people said "Amen," and I retired to my seat. The situation was saved, but my conscience troubled me. I felt that I must tell someone, so the following week at the W. M. S. meeting I told what I had done. It was a great relief to have the women laugh heartily, all agreeing I could scarcely have done otherwise.

On a certain furlough I brought home about seventy good lantern slides on our work in North Honan. After some rather trying experiences, I came to see it was imperative that certain conditions should be fulfilled to insure a successful lantern evening. The following experiences show that success depends largely on these conditions:

First essential—a good lantern.
Second essential—an expert operator.
Third essential—lantern, screen, etc., to be in place at least half an hour before meeting time, when slides should be tested as to *perfect focus*.
Fourth essential—the entire program should be in command of the lecturer.

Just two outstanding experiences are given by way of contrast and to illustrate the importance of these essentials.

Receiving a most hearty, even urgent, request for my lantern lecture to be given during an important woman's missionary convention in M— (one of the largest and most important cities of the Dominion), I wrote back saying

I would come only on condition a promise would be given me that they agree to the things mentioned. The reply was satisfactory. All would be arranged as I wished.

On reaching M—, a few hours before the meeting was to take place, my hostess seemed very uneasy. Finally she said, "I fear you will be disappointed, Mrs. Goforth. Some of the women on the committee were afraid you might disappoint them, so a regular program has been arranged; and though it was supposed just to supplement you, it is quite long. I really don't know when you will get a start!" It would be easier for one to imagine, than for me to describe, my feelings on hearing this. When I learned that the renowned Dr. Pringle, of the Yukon, was to give an address *before* me, I phoned those responsible and did my utmost to give up my part. But I had to submit; there was no way out, except that I remained absolutely firm on one point: Dr. Pringle must follow, not precede me.

It was a few moments after eight o'clock when we reached the church, which was packed to the doors. With difficulty we made our way to a front seat. A glance about was sufficient to confirm my fears: a long, *flat* church and an immense sounding board over the pulpit spoke eloquently of poor acoustics. But, worst of all, the curtain was so arranged that when swung across it would come to the *outer edge of the platform and within three feet of the front seats.* Almost in a state of panic, I begged a woman to bring the minister to me. He came, looking none too pleased.

I said, "Dr.—, where am I to stand?"

For a moment he looked rather nonplussed. Then he said, "We'll get a chair. You can stand on it!"

He turned away, but I could not let him go without one more effort. "But Dr. _____, the church is *flat*, the people will neither see nor hear me. Do at least ask the women to remove their Merry Widow hats!"

But the old gentleman declined and left me. There was nothing more I could do. I seated myself in the front pew with a feeling of despair and waited for things to take their course.

The program, as arranged by the women, went on its way till considerably after nine o'clock. Then the curtain was drawn across, falling, as I had feared, at the outer edge of the platform. A *small* chair was brought and placed with its back touching the curtain. Two men kindly came forward and lifted me on to the chair before that great audience! One of them, noticing how shaky I was, kept hold of me until I was able to balance myself. But to my horror, I almost fell off the chair again and again when I tried to turn so as to get a glimpse of the picture on the screen. Then the final failure began. The lantern, far back on the gallery, was hopelessly out of focus. Even I had the utmost difficulty in making out what a picture was meant to be. This was not once, nor twice, but all the pictures were the same. How I got through those seventy slides, I never could tell, but at last *with help* I descended from my perch. By this time half the audience had left. It was ten o'clock or after when Dr. Pringle took the platform.

I do hope all who have read the foregoing will not fail to read the following:

Some weeks after that (to me) truly terrible experience in M— (I trembled for days after), I was asked to give the same lecture in Winnipeg. In this case each stipulated condition was fully met. I ascended the platform of Dr. C. W. Gordon's church to face one of the finest audiences it has ever been my privilege to address. The Winnipeg Presbytery had come over in a body; the keen appreciation shown by the ministers' repeated applause did much to make the evening an outstanding success. But nevertheless the slides were the same and my talk was the same as in M—. At the close of the lecture, a second and impromptu collection was taken up, and one hundred dollars was given to me as a personal gift. This later was put to the purchase of an organ for China.

We were on furlough at the time of the Great War. An invitation reached us from Dr. and Mrs. Talling, old friends, to attend a musicale at their home. I went alone, as Dr. Goforth was out of the city. Arriving rather late, I slipped into the one vacant seat near the door, for a solo was in progress. Just as it was ending, Dr. Talling came to me and whispered, "Nearly everyone is taking part. Now, what will you do?"

Without a thought of him taking me seriously, I replied laughingly, "Put me down for 'Tipperary' in Chinese."

The woman beside me heard what I said and,

jumping to her feet, ran to the piano and started to play "Tipperary" in brilliant fashion. At the same time Dr. Talling announced, while drawing me forward, "Mrs. Goforth will now favor us with 'Tipperary' in Chinese."

What could I do? I had no time even to get panicky when I found myself beside the piano. The accompanist nodded for me to begin. With a feeling akin to "I'll go through with it if I die in the attempt," I drew myself up and sang out with full voice, then repeated softly as I felt within the tenderness of that chorus and what it had meant to our soldiers. Well, I can only say the response was great, but I dared not respond to the encore!

As the gathering was breaking up, a woman came to me, saying, "Why, Mrs. Goforth, I did not know you were so musical. Do you have many musical advantages in China?"

When I endeavored to enlighten her on this point, she was most sympathetic. Several months passed; then shortly before returning to China I received a letter from this woman telling of a new Victrola with a number of records having been packed ready to accompany us to China, the gift of herself and her husband. So I never regretted my only appearance in public as a soloist. And what a blessing that Victrola was not only to ourselves but others!

In *Goforth of China* I have already told of our first journey across the Pacific in the notorious "Parthia," notorious for its excessive "heaving, pitching, and rolling."

As we left that boat, I registered a silent but solemn vow that nothing, no nothing, could ever induce me to set foot on that vessel again—but alas for my vow!

Several years later, when I was returning to China alone with several children, passage was taken on the "Victoria" from Seattle, Washington. Four days out to sea, I made my first appearance in the dining room. Addressing the purser, by whom I was seated, I said, "Purser, his boat is simply terrible! It puts me in mind of the old 'Parthia,' for its rolling, pitching, and heaving." I then told of the first journey to China and my vow, whereupon the purser laughed so loudly all eyes were turned to our table.

When able to speak, he said, "Well, Mrs. Goforth, I'm sorry to tell you you've broken your vow. This is the old 'Parthia.' She was taken over to Glasgow, cut in two, considerable added to her length, renamed 'Victoria,' and returned to the Pacific by a different line."

An incident occurred when I was traveling by the trans-Siberian route to China from England, which was nothing short of tragic to the writer.

We had to change cars many times and were impressed with the richness of the Russian trains. On one train the compartment we occupied was upholstered in the richest pale green plush, even to the floor rug. As the train meals were very expensive and we had five children with us, I tried to lessen the expense by getting at least our breakfast. Our compartment was, as can be imagined, fairly crowded with seven in it.

One morning, as I was endeavoring to pour

thick, condensed coffee milk into a cup, one of the children accidentally knocked my arm with such force that the tin was sent flying, its contents scattering everywhere over the rich, silk plush. My first thought was, "What will the porter say?" We were to leave the train in an hour, so there was no time to be lost. While my husband took charge of the children in the hallway and did his best to clean the coffee from their clothes, I worked frantically (this is not too strong a word) with hot water to get the coffee stains out of the plush, but work as I would, I only partially succeeded. How I wished we could have traveled sensibly C. P. R. tourist style. It was a guilty party that left the train that day.

Chapter XI

MISSIONARY MODES

Fools for Christ's sake.—The Apostle Paul.

I wonder how many who may read these pages have heard the expression, "Those dowdy missionaries!" or how many, even on certain occasions, have had the expression forced from themselves?

Now, I know in writing as I am about to do, there will be danger of giving offense to some. All missionaries are not dowdy, and none, I believe, really wish to be so. Some are even quite *dressy!* It is, however, a fact that many missionaries are quite misunderstood because of what may be called their "modes."

I have been urged to tell something of my own experience in the matter of dress when returning to the homeland. I do so, not because the stories are somewhat amusing, but chiefly that through these incidents the reader may better understand why missionaries find it difficult to adopt modes that will satisfy and please all critical eyes when on platforms or elsewhere in the homelands.

On our first furlough I purchased a dark green velvet toque, with just one ornament—a very dainty yellow osprey. When wearing that toque, I always faced an audience with the feeling that my appearance was "beyond reproach," but, alas, my pride had a fall when toward the end of the winter a woman came up to my husband and said: "Why do you allow your wife to wear that green toque? She is doing a great deal of harm. People think it very wrong for her to wear that osprey!" Of course I felt very bad when told this because of my having been a stumbling block. I had a good cry, and, of course, the osprey was destroyed, leaving my unadorned toque decidedly *dowdy*.

During the following furlough a deputation of two waited on me immediately on our arrival in Toronto. They came from the ladies of a certain church, which had chosen them to fit me out completely at their expense. After my experience on our previous furlough, I was greatly relieved that the responsibility of choosing my mode should be on others. So the three of us went downtown. (I may just remark here that I was not far beyond thirty.)

The first article chosen was a perfectly plain, but good, black dress; the second, a black *cape,* with wide silk ribbon heavily box-pleated around the neck. The cape was tied with a generous bow of ribbon of the same width, with two long ends hanging down. We then went to the millinery department. Of course I left myself entirely in the hands of my friends. A beautiful *bonnet* of rich, black silk, black flowers, and ribbon was chosen. It fastened by a heavy black ribbon bow with long ends. But it was the *height* of the bonnet that startled me and gave me a sense of uneasiness. My old hat and coat were left to be sent home, and I put on the bonnet and cape. On reaching home, my husband and all the children met me at the door. On catching sight of my new outfit, Dr. Goforth exclaimed in an awe-stricken voice: "Why, Rose, what on earth have you got on? You look like an old woman!"

"Please don't find fault with the things," I replied, "I'll have to wear them, for all the money is spent." Well, dear friends, I did wear that bonnet and cape several months, perforce. Then one day, I was traveling by train with my four children. A woman on the opposite side of the train rose and, coming over to me, said: "I have been so interested in watching you and your lovely *grandchildren!*" This was too much! I thought, "It's the bonnet." On returning to Toronto, I went at once and bought a simple and inexpensive toque, of which I have never heard, fortunately, any adverse criticism.

Returning to Canada in the early summer of 1916, my husband was so seriously ill he was quite unable to do any public speaking. I had found it very difficult to get anything like even a passable outfit for the journey. I had secured a black sailor hat, which was all the style then. With pictures of hats trimmed with black silk bows high and *very upright,* I suceeded after considerable trouble in trimming the hat, making three bows remain upright by sewing them on to steel hairpins, which had been straightened out.

So I trimmed the hat to my entire satisfaction, and all who saw it on me admired it, till I became quite vain.

We reached Vancouver late Saturday night, when all stores were closed. A telephone message came saying Dr. Goforth was booked to speak Sunday night at a certain church (one of the largest in Vancouver). As he could not go, I had to take his place.

Naturally, before leaving for the church that Sunday night, I admired to the full my quite stylish, self-trimmed hat, with the thought, "Well, at least they won't say I'm *dowdy!*" The church was packed. Up to a certain point, I seemed to hold the audience. Then something happened. There were strange looks that came over the faces—startled, surprised, amused, and even amazed expressions. I could not understand the meaning of it, not till I walked rather proudly up to the looking glass on reaching my own room. Then to my horror and disgust I saw that the three ribbon bows had fallen flat, *leaving the three hairpins standing upright alone!*

Oh, the humiliation of it! I could almost hear voices saying, "Oh, those awful missionaries! Why don't they dress decently?" Little did that audience know how keenly I had wanted to at least "pass muster!"

Many China missionaries could, no doubt, tell stories of getting suits made by Chinese tailors in Shanghai, which *there* were considered quite passable, but would be considered "impossible" when the home circle was reached.

On one occasion I had such a suit made and

wore it with the utmost satisfaction, unconscious of criticism, until a frank friend told me, after arrival in Toronto, "You cannot possibly go to church in such a thing!" That suit was laid away carefully and met the fate on our return to China a year later of being cut up into wee boy's panties.

Though many stories, both amusing and tragic, could be told along the same line, these will suffice. Those who have the understanding heart will, I trust, be able to read in these experiences some of the problems "modes" present to missionaries who are preparing to face the critical "home" eyes accustomed to ever-changing fashions.

May I close this chapter with a wee "call back" message especially for returned or returning missionaries! It is this: *Pray for guidance about your clothes!* Since I began to do this, I have never been *openly* criticized, and I have had many experiences when it seemed the Lord had very definitely guided. I will give just one concrete case.

When I was on furlough, a friend (who had a very strong will) insisted on choosing a hat for me. I did not like it, but to please her, I yielded. On returning home, I became convinced that it would be *very wrong* for me to wear it. Others could wear such a hat, but I simply could not. And my money for a hat was gone!

Having an old shape and a piece of good velvet, I shut myself in my room, and, after praying the Lord to guide my hands, I pinned the velvet onto the shape. When it was finished, I went to my daughter with it on. "O Mother!" she cried, "it is just perfect. I wouldn't change it!" What a comfort that toque was, and I knew the Lord had guided!

> There is nothing too small for His love,
> And nothing too great for His power.

CHAPTER XII

BEAUTIFUL PEITAIHO

He giveth us richly all things to enjoy.

TOWARD THE CLOSE of the last century a Tientsin missionary, when touring with his evangelist, discovered Peitaiho. Standing on high vantage ground, he marveled at the beauty and the grandeur of the scene before him—a vast, rolling valley with ranges of mountains to the north and west, and to the south the blue waters of the Pacific beating against five miles of coast line which continued on at a sharp angle three miles eastward to the point where the Great Wall of China meets the ocean.

As the missionary gazed upon the scene, there came to him the inspiration that later brought blessing and relief to multitudes: "What an ideal place for a health resort." Hastening to Tientsin, he called a meeting of the missionaries and told what he had found. The matter was taken up enthusiastically. Before 1900 with its wholesale destruction came, cottages dotted the entire Peitaiho coast line. This was the beginning. In a few years Peitaiho came to be the greatest summer resort of the Far East.

In company with many other interior missionaries with children, my husband and I hailed with eagerness the opportunity of securing a place of refuge for the children from the great heat of inland China, lasting through at least six weeks in midsummer. Two of our children had died during the hottest season.

We were among the first to get a cottage. The site was on high ground facing the eastern shore. But it was scarcely completed when the Boxers destroyed every cottage in the Peitaiho region. Two years later the place was rebuilt, and for fifteen years our cottage was an untold blessing to us as a family, though my husband was rarely able to spend much time with us.

Here the children, who were being educated at the China Inland Mission schools at Chefoo (just across the gulf), were able to spend their summer holidays with us.

Weather permitting, our dining table was placed on a wide, north veranda. Here, for six days in the week, I gave the mornings to sewing, with a small hand-machine, which always accompanied us from Changte. The children's school outfits had to be replenished. I felt it important to get as much sewing done as possible during the summer holidays so as to be free for women's work later. Thirty to forty garments made during the summer holidays were my usual quota.

Sitting on the veranda at my work, I faced one of the most beautiful views in the world. World travelers have told us it reminded them of the Bay of Naples. From the veranda, we had an unbroken view of both sunset and sunrise, the former dipping behind gorgeous ranges of mountains, the latter rising out of the ocean.

One experience I shall never forget. It had been a very hot night. I had risen about midnight and had lain on a hammock outside. Very early I awoke, thinking the whole place was on fire. When I looked about me, I saw the whole heavens, sea, and land ablaze with a strange, crimson glow. It was all beautiful, yet awesome. I ran into the house to arouse the family, but all continued their sleep except a young woman visitor.

As we came out together, the brilliant, crimson glow was beginning, on mountain and sea, to be touched with gold. The glory of the scene was such that we just sank on our knees, till gradually, as the sun began to herald itself, the glory passed. After that experience, I could understand a little the words: "The glory of the Lord had filled the house of God." [1]

The following unexplainable incident took place at the time the Peitaiho railway station was situated well back, several miles from the coast line. Our cottage was six miles distant, and the intervening roads were—well, quite indescribable! They would have to be endured to be understood. Corduroy roads in the Canadian bush, sixty years ago, were comfortable in comparison. I know, for I experienced a ride on one once!

One summer I arrived at the Peitaiho station with several children. Our boxes of stores were in the freight shed, where I was taken to sign some papers. Taking off my long distance glasses to write, they were laid on a box and forgotten.

---

[1] II Chron. 5:14.

They were not missed till late the following day. How I prayed that the glasses might be kept safe! The next morning a messenger was dispatched to the station master, with the faint hope that they might have been found. A few hours later the messenger returned with the following extraordinary story:

When half way home from the station (the station master knew nothing of the glasses) the messenger had met a friend. When he told of his failure to get my glasses, the man said: "I have them!" He then told how, the day before, as he walked along the cart road, he spied a pair of glasses almost hidden by a bush, that had evidently jolted off a cart. The glasses were brought to me unbroken—just slightly bent! Knowing the roughness with which Chinese coolies handle boxes, the keenness they have for anything foreign, the roughness of the roads, and the violent jolting of the springless carts, the way the glasses had been preserved and then held by the friend of our servant, all seemed wonderful. How could I help but believe God had again answered prayer?

It would be difficult indeed to tabulate the blessings of Peitaiho. The place came to be called "The Children's Paradise," and many a missionary went up to Peitaiho broken in health and a few weeks later was able to return to his station strengthened in body and spiritually refreshed for further service. On one occasion I reached Peitaiho so weak as to be unable to walk without assistance. Within two weeks I was roaming the hills and seashore and drinking in the truly life-giving breezes of that wonderful place.

The children's greatest treat was donkey-riding. How they did enjoy making those donkeys go, with the boy owners flying after them! My husband was like a boy again when donkey-cantering with the children. But not so the writer, who could scarcely get a donkey strong enough to hold her safely.

The following is an incident which in more ways than one made a lasting impression on me. There was to be a large picnic over on the Lotus Hill, four or five miles west of our home. As usual, when it came time for choosing donkeys, one after another of the donkey boys managed to elude my husband as he tried to secure a good, strong animal for me, for each boy sought a light load and I was—well, the heaviest in sight.

At last all were off but our two selves and two *small* donkeys. After considerable maneuvering and help, I succeeded in getting on my donkey's back and started off. When a few yards from the house, the brute suddenly stretched out his hind legs, which cause me to slide off gently to the ground standing! A second attempt was made. This time, when but a few feet from the house, the animal stopped short, dipped his head, and bent his knees to a kneeling position, which caused me to take a most undignified position on the ground, unhurt, except for my feelings. By this time I saw fire in my husband's eyes. He said, "Try the brute once more." I did, but though the donkey boy pulled and my husband pushed, the donkey refused to take a step. Then, as if suddenly awakening to a new stunt, he let his legs go from under him and rested his whole body on the ground. As soon as I had extricated myself from the animal, my husband and I looked at each other completely beaten. At last I said, "Let me try yours." Now, whether this second donkey, which had been a quiet witness of all that was going on, decided to behave itself, who knows? But the fact is it turned out to be as gentle and docile as a lamb.

All went well for some miles, my husband following behind on the very donkey that had refused me. The Lotus Hills were reached safely and we could see through the trees the rest of the party far up the hill. By this time, I had become elated at riding successfully so far. Just as we were coming to a small rivulet, I turned slightly and called to my husband, close behind, "Look, Jonathan, see how well I ride. I will soon be able to compete with the children."

At that instant the donkey gave a sudden spring, and I found myself sitting in the middle of the stream! No more need be said except that my return journey that day was made in a more dignified mode of travel, by chair. From then on, except on rare occasions, I enjoyed donkey-riding by proxy.

A deeper note should now be sounded!

One summer at our Women's Conference, made up entirely of women missionaries, married and single, a woman rose and said (as near as I can quote her words):

"We mothers have heard with mixed feelings

of Mrs. Goforth's going with her husband on his country tours and of her taking her children with her. I should like to ask Mrs. Goforth a question, in the name of other mothers, as well as myself, who want to do God's will—but we do fear for our children. My question is: Have your children suffered as the result of such a life? We hear five of your children have died."

Rising, I replied: "I am most thankful for the opportunity to answer this question. The five children who have gone before all died *before* I began the touring life. Since I began that life, two children have been given us. Further, I have found the children happier and healthier than before. I have found it possible to give actually more time to them than before, for the time necessarily given to keeping up a foreign house may, when outside, be given to the children. I can truly say I know of no harm that has come to any during these eight or nine years of that life. Not one has contracted any infectious disease and, best of all, God has set His seal upon this plan of work by giving a harvest of souls everywhere we have gone."

One further little memory of that dear old Peitaiho home. I had been in poor health. The doctors told my husband they strongly advised my returning to Canada. In the meantime, I was to rest. So, making myself comfortable on a bed-hammock on the veranda, I called for a book. Someone brought me *Mary Slessor of Calabar*, with the remark, "You can at least glance through it; you would not care to wade through it all."

I began at the beginning. Each page increased my sense of thrill at such a character! Such a life! Not a word could I miss. Never had I read anything that had so gripped my highest ideals. After two days, I came to the place where Mary Slessor, at fifty-four, in poor health, was urged to return to Scotland to the loving welcome awaiting her and to her well-earned rest. Oh, how my heart thrilled as I went on. For only a brief moment she hesitated—was it to be rest in Scotland or Calabar! The decision was made, and at fifty-four she turned her face toward the life that made her one of the greatest heroines the world has ever known.

I could go no farther just then. I, too, was fifty-four years of age and facing the order to return home. How dare I in the face of what I had just read? Praise God, grace and strength came with the new vision, and I obeyed. How wonderfully the Lord sustained in the long, strenuous journeys that began less than a month later!

Little did we dream that autumn as we left our hilltop cottage that it was to be a final farewell.

The nomadic life such as we were about to enter upon had its compensations. We met from time to time, as briefly as *ships that pass in the night,* personalities that left upon us inspiring impressions that never faded. We came to hear first hand testimonies to the mighty power of God, which enriched our lives, strengthened our faith, and sent us on, better able to help others.

Our journeyings often led us through some of

the most beautiful regions of China. One memory comes of the scenery we passed through when making a five-day journey by chair through Hunan and Kiangsi. These provinces lie side by side and are so joined by waterways and ranges of mountains and hills as to be separate chiefly in name. The population of the region is said to be about half that of the United States. For days we passed through scenes of grandeur and rare beauty. Never had we seen such rich and varied coloring in nature. Much of the soil is a deep red and appears in great strips down the mountain-sides, giving the effect from a distance of vast flower gardens. Quite frequently beautiful combinations of trees were seen. The most striking of these was the heavy, wide-spreading, dark green, almost black camphor tree, with tall, stately pines close by, and between was the soft, feathery, pale green of the young bamboo trees. Then, lower down in the valley, was the emerald green of the rice fields, with here and there a patch of gold—the fields of mustard.

In our journeyings through this region, we were constantly reminded of the lines:

> Where every prospect pleases
> And only man is vile.

Frequently after we traveled through scenes such as I have endeavored to picture, changing with every step of our rapid-pacing chair-bearers, a sudden, sharp turn of the road would bring us into a village street where uncovered cesspools abounded by the roadside, causing us to cover our faces and hold our breath in horror till we were again in God's unpolluted air.

CHAPTER XIII

TREASURED MEMORIES

God uses human channels
To reach human hearts.
                    —*S. D. Gordon*

How an Old Woman Was Won by a Sketch

A CROSS, crabbed, old creature whose face resembled a piece of crinkled brown paper, with two holes through which sharp, black eyes looked you through and through! No wonder she had earned the name, "Old Autocrat"! For more than twenty years this woman had experienced to the full her power and authority as senior over the entire Chang clan, whose numbers were legion.

The old woman was indeed a character. Only the pen of a Charles Dickens could do her justice. For twenty years she had been a widow, living alone in her two-room house. When her husband died, she had her own coffin made and placed in a safe place—just outside her bedroom window! It was supported from the ground by bricks and covered carefully with many layers of straw mats. Her two rooms contained an indescribable conglomeration of things she regarded as treasures—crocks of every size and degree of imperfection, stuffed with old, worn-out things that emitted a far from pleasant odor.

The one place always kept clean and tidy was the brick platform bed in the inner room. Neatly folded quilts of bright colors were always in evidence. The tiny brick stove built against the kang carried welcome warmth into the hollow, brick bed.

Yes, the Old Autocrat was indeed a real character. For more than a year, I had utterly failed even to get a glimpse of her, for she feared one look from me would mesmerize her. Then one day, when we were spending some days preaching in the village, one of the younger members of the family with whom we were staying said to me: "Oh, I do wish you could win our old grandmother, the Autocrat. She is making it so hard for us Christians. Everyone fears her tongue. Many would come out and join us, but they are afraid of her, for she hates Christians."

As she was speaking, a sudden thought came to me, and, turning to my dear Bible woman, in whom I had complete confidence, I said, "Mrs. Wang, please go over to the old woman's door and try to get in touch with her while we stay here and pray." Off went Mrs. Wang as quickly as her poor, crippled feet could carry her. Reaching the old woman's door, she knocked several times with no response. She knew the Old Autocrat was within, for the two-leafed door was barred inside. Just as Mrs. Wang was about to turn away, she heard the bar being drawn aside and then very slowly the door was opened, just a little.

"What do you want?" came gruffly from inside.

"I just want to pay my respects to you, my venerable grandmother," said Mrs. Wang, sweetly.

"I know what you have come for, just to talk against my gods," was the sharp retort.

"No, indeed," said Mrs. Wang quickly. "I'll not say a word about your gods; I'll only talk about mine, if you let me in."

This seemed to please the old woman. The door opened, and she and Mrs. Wang began talking about *me*. Later I was amused at the highly colored picture she drew of me, but it succeeded in rousing the old woman's curiosity. Before long, she exclaimed, "Do you think she will come over if I invite her?"

Scarcely able to hide her elation, Mrs. Wang replied, "I think she would, if I went for her."

A few moments later we were all startled by my Mrs. Wang bursting breathlessly into our midst, saying, "Come quickly, the Old Autocrat has invited you over."

We all started at once, and on reaching the old woman's home I was surprised at the warmth of her reception. But inborn fear was evidently struggling with equally inborn courtesy. The latter won as she placed, for me, one of the least rickety of her chairs. Almost immediately, the old lady opened fire. "Do you mean to tell me those eyes do not see me?" she asked, pointing to a hideous picture representing the god of wealth.

Realizing the need for great care in dealing with this strange old character, I replied, "Do you really think they can see you?"

"Of course they can! And those, and those," pointing to pictures of several minor gods.

Before replying, I raised a cry for wisdom, and then said: "Venerable grandmother, do you think I can make eyes that can see?"

"You! Certainly not," she replied emphatically.

"Then," I said; "if I make eyes that *seem* to look at you far more really than any of these gods, and make them on paper like these gods are printed on, will you, my venerable grandmother, believe that these eyes, which you *think* can see you, are only picture eyes that *seem* to see?"

For several moments we faced each other, looking straight into each other's eyes, while the crowd around us waited with bated breath. Then the old woman tossed her head, and with a laugh of victory said, "Ah, but you can't."

"You just see," I replied quickly. "Wait here; I'll be back in a few moments." Away I flew (or tried to) through two courts and down an alleyway to my room, where I found my husband reading his Bible.

"Oh, quick, Jonathan," I cried, "get me a red and blue pencil, a fountain pen, a lead, and an indelible pencil." While he was gathering these together, I told him what I was about to do. Then, catching up a large, unruled writing pad and the pencils, I hastened back.

The crowd had greatly increased. The room

was so packed I could scarcely find elbowroom. Then, placing the old woman close beside me so she could see every line I drew, I started to draw.

Many years before, my father had taught me to draw a human face by rule. These rules I determined to follow. As my pencils flew, the interest increased till the crowd swayed back and forth in their effort to see what I was doing. When the first rough outline was finished, I tinted the cheeks and lips with red pencil, colored the garment with the blue, and the hair black with the fountain pen; but the final touches were to the eyes. While putting these to the eyes, I kept praying the Lord to help me make them lifelike. When the last touch was given, I felt startled, the eyes were so lifelike.

"Oh, give it to me, give it to me!" cried the old woman, trying to grasp the picture from me.

"No, no," I replied; "you cannot have it unless you promise not to worship it." Then, making my way to where the god of wealth was pasted on the wall, I held my picture close beside the horrible, distorted face of the god, the eyes of which, strange to say, looked very lifelike. The old woman had followed me closely.

"Now, venerable grandmother," I said, so that all could hear, "which pair of eyes *seem* to look at you most really? Speak truthfully." The old woman remained silent for a few moments while a great stillness reigned in the room. Then, with a great soblike sigh, a catch in her voice, and a look in her eyes which was half-frightened and half-awakened, she stretched out her hand, saying, beggingly: "Say no more, lady. Give me the picture, and I will promise not to worship it." I gave it to her with a gentle pressure. I could see the old woman had been under great strain. And what wonder! To have the deeply rooted beliefs of almost eighty years destroyed in a few brief moments!

As I turned to leave, a woman in the crowd called out, "Perhaps you don't know, lady, what a *hao chao hua-ti* our old grandmother is [being interpreted, the Chinese means *a connoisseur in art*]."

"Oh, are you?" I asked, turning to the old grandmother. "Then we shall be great friends, for I am a connoisseur in art, too! I have lots of pictures, and every time I come to Changte I shall try to remember to bring you one." So, in the months that followed, many a brilliant picture, cut out of illustrated papers supplied us by friends at home, found its way to the Old Autocrat's walls, gradually replacing the execrable pictures that had for long covered the walls and had earned for her the reputation of being a collector of art!

The spiritual change that came in this strange but lovable old woman was slow but steady, but for more than a year the villagers had continued reason to fear her tongue. Her devotion to us both was touching in the extreme. When visiting the village, she allowed no one but herself to entertain us. It did, at first, give me a creepy feeling to think of that coffin so close, just a few inches away! As the influence of the Gospel came to gain its power over her, she seemed to lose interest in the coffin.

The time came when my husband and I were away from the Changte region for five years. On our return, we once more paid a visit to the Old Autocrat's village. As we entered the little church, the first thing to catch my eye was the old woman's coffin resting in a prominent place just beside the preacher's desk. Turning to the evangelist in charge, I said, "Mr. Li, you surely are not going to let *that thing* remain there?"

With a surprised look, he replied: "Why not, lady? It's empty!"

Not being able to give a satisfactory answer to the "why," the coffin remained as a convenient resting-place for Bible and hymn books.

The time came when we must bid farewell to our dear, old Changte field. Shortly before the tearing up began, old Mrs. Chang, for we can no more call her "Old Autocrat," appeared at our door. What a delight she took in examining everything from the kitchen stove to the globe in my husband's study!

But what seemed to fascinate her most were the pictures. Again and again she turned to them. As we stood together looking at a beautiful water-color drawing of snow-capped Rocky Mountain peaks which my artist brother had given me many years before, I saw a strange (to me), beautiful wistfulness on the old woman's face. The thought of the chrysalis came—how it was shut up in its hard, uncomely crust till the time of its deliverance. So, I thought, this old woman, with her instinctive love for the beautiful, has been enclosed and imprisoned in the hard, unbroken crust of heathen environment.

But the grace of God had begun to work, and the time of her deliverance was at hand, when she would come forth unfettered and beautiful to ascend to the God who made her.

Who knows but that some day you and I shall meet her in the glory land who was once known as the Old Autocrat—a beautiful soul, changed into His image!

The Wolf-Boy and His Mother

A lad about fourteen years of age named Cheng (surname) Wootsi (given name) left his home in Changte city to visit his aunt in the mountainous region to the west. It was winter, and the wolves were causing terror in the villages.

Wootsi, as we shall call him, when on a message up the village street, was attacked by a great wolf. Before it could be driven off, the poor boy's face was terribly mangled. For months the ignorant villagers did what they could for the lad, but when it seemed the boy would die, he was brought to our mission hospital. The case was a most unusual one. For almost a year he remained in the hospital, tenderly nursed by his mother, who was a widow and devotedly attached to her boy.

The doctor spoke of it as the most difficult case he had ever had. For many months, the process of grafting was carried on, which proved only partially successful. One eye was saved and a new mouth formed. But when all was done that could be done, the boy's face still remained such

a horrible spectacle he was obliged to wear a
mask.

While in the hospital, the poor, torn lad had
won the hearts of all by his gratitude for every
kindness, his cheerfulness and patience under
suffering, and his simple, loving nature. The
hearts of both mother and son were opened to
the Gospel message by the kindness shown them,
and both became Christians.

Our little band of Christians were startled and
deeply moved at the weekly prayer meeting one
evening when Wootsi rose and prayed, as follows: "O Lord, I thank Thee for letting the wolf
eat my face. If this had not happened, I might
never have heard of this wonderful Saviour."

Later Wootsi was given the humble position
of water carrier for the mission station, for the
missionaries felt it would be the height of cruelty
to turn the poor lad adrift to the "tender mercies
of the heathen." In spite of his terrible handicap,
he became beloved by all, even the foreign children.

Never can I forget the boy's sympathy and sorrow when our precious, golden-haired Florence
was stricken unto death. For days and days the
lad waited outside the bedroom door every moment he could get from his work, praying for the
word of hope that was not to come. When at last
he was told the spirit of the child was no longer
with us, his heartbroken grief was touching to
witness.

About the time Wootsi became our water carrier, I was greatly in need of an *amah* for the
children. I had been praying for one, the right

one, to be sent to me—above all else a woman with whom I could trust the children, for often the work among the women necessitated my absence from home for many hours at a time. During the last year Mrs. Cheng waited on her son in the hospital, I had often been impressed with her tenderness and patience. To help her out with the hospital expenses, we had her work for us some hours each day. It was not long before she had won the love of all. On Wootsi's leaving the hospital, she came to us as a permanent nurse.

A year later came that terrible cataclysm of horror, the Boxer uprising. To face the long journey southward to Hankow by cart with small children and *without Mrs. Cheng* was to me appalling. But would she, could she come? We laid our need before her. For one day, she hesitated, going about the house as if dazed.

At evening, she came with tears, saying, "Oh, my Shepherd Mother, I must go with you. My old mother [eighty] weeps, but says I must go. My boy needs me, for his face still needs dressing, but he too tells me to go, *for the children need me most!"*

Weeks of terrible experience followed.[1] Through all, Mrs. Cheng proved herself an untold blessing to us all. Twice she was tested as few have ever been, but how nobly she stood the test! On that terrible eleventh day, when it seemed all were to be massacred, this wonderful woman, when separated with little Ruth from

---

[1] *Goforth of China,* chapter X.

the rest of us and attacked by men demanding the child, lay down, covering the little one and taking blow after blow upon herself. By the mercy of God, they were both saved, as their assailants turned to get their share of the loot.

That night, about 2:00 A.M., our whole party was again facing seemingly certain death. Several Chinese came to Mrs. Cheng, begging her to leave us and save herself. They even promised to have her taken safely back to her home at Changte, but she refused. It was a very dark night. We had no lamp nor candles. Suddenly I heard a sound of weeping outside. Following the sound, I found Mrs. Cheng sitting alone on a narrow veranda, weeping bitterly and moaning aloud: "I must go. I must go. Even if they kill me, I must go!" As I sat down beside her, we clung to each other in our distress.

Then a strange thing happened. Two Chinese women, creeping along the wall, appeared through the darkness, and, on reaching us, knelt down before us and began to weep. Almost too surprised for words, I said, "Are you Christians?"

"We don't understand," was the reply.

"Then why have you come for us now?"

"Because our hearts feel sorry for you." These words but inadequately convey their beautiful, touching sympathy, for, as I have said, tears were in their eyes, and their looks and manners meant more than words. But before I had time to say more than a few words to them, the call came to get into our carts.

During those terrible days that followed, when we almost starved, when sickness came first to one, then to another, when all were exhausted and tried to the last point of endurance, Mrs. Cheng, through it all, thought not one moment of herself but only of those she served.

When at last Shanghai was reached and the parting came, we to go to Canada, and Mrs. Cheng to the care of our friends in Chefoo, quite a party escorted the beloved nurse to the coast steamer. As the last, tearful farewells outside her cabin door were ended, the dear woman drew me aside and sobbingly said: "Oh, my lady, *do take good care of the children!*" As we parted, smiles were mixed with tears.

The Story of the Tatungfu Mission

Of whom the world was not worthy.[2]

While we were on our vacation at Peitaiho in the summer of 1932, an urgent call came for my husband to hold revival meetings at Tatungfu, an important city in North Shansi. The invitation had come from the Swedish Missions of that region, which were affiliated with the China Inland Mission.

The journey was a long and expensive one, and I had been urged to accompany my husband. Dr. Goforth and I decided we would ask the Lord to send us sufficient to meet all traveling expenses, for we did not wish those dear "faith" missionaries to be put to any expense by our coming. Shortly before we were to leave for Tatungfu, a letter was received from a woman in America enclosing a check amply sufficient

---

[2] Heb. 11:38.

to cover our travel. The donor said, "This is for yourselves to be used in any way you think fit." It was indeed a gift *timed of the Lord,* a blessed seal of God upon the coming mission. We went forward with a sense of joyful assurance of the Lord's being with us.

How can I write of the two weeks spent among those sorely tried, faithful, isolated Swedish brethren and sisters and the hundred and fifty Chinese leaders who gathered for the meetings! As I recall those days they seem almost too sacred to record.

I was humbled and brought low before the Lord when I found my part in the mission was to be an hour each morning with the forty or more missionaries. What could I give them? How could I help them? The deeply lived life in Christ was revealed in every face. All I dared do was just to tell simply what the Lord had done for me. Rarely if ever have I felt the Lord's upholding and presence more than while in fellowship with those simple, earnest, seeking souls, most of whom were from lonely, isolated centers with not more than two or three in a station.

Never had we been in any part of China where the tragic side of missionary life was more in evidence. During the Boxer uprising, every missionary—man, woman, and child—of the Swedish Mission, also many Christians, were martyred. We were taken to what they called "The Sacred Spot," a Chinese courtyard in the center of the city. While we were standing together in the court, the woman missionary in charge of a girls' school there told us how in that very court in 1900 six missionaries and four children were cruelly put to death. As I listened to some of the awful details, a deathly faintness overcame me. Miss B., seeing this, laid her hand on my shoulder, saying, "Take comfort, Mrs. Goforth, I have a wonderful thing to tell you." She then told of how five years after the Boxer troubles she had opened a girls' school in the court. One day some of the children, poking in a heap of rubbish in a corner of the court, discovered a small, English, pocket Testament. It was almost falling to pieces and the printing indecipherable, but when it was brought to Miss B., she found the following words alone stood out quite clearly:

Of whom the world was not worthy
—Heb. 11:38

How wonderful that just these words should have stood the storms of five years that the Lord himself might speak through His own Word of the glories of those who suffered martyrdom for His name's sake!

We were told that, even at the time of our visit, an average of four missionaries died yearly in that region of typhoid fever or were killed by bandits.

The senior lady missionary attending the conference told me in broken English some truly remarkable stories of how the Lord had answered prayer for her. Some of these I took notes of at the time. I will give just one, believing it will help others as it did me.

In the spring of 1900 she and her husband and

several children were in Stockholm. All preparations had been made for their return to China when a cable came telling of all their missionaries having been killed by the Boxers. All their money had been spent on an outfit for China. A time of great testing came. One day the young servant girl came to Mrs. H., saying, "There are no more potatoes." They practically lived on potatoes. Mrs. H. began to cry, saying, "I have no money. We will starve." Again, she gave way to sobbing. The young girl laid her hand gently upon her, and said, "Mrs. H., don't cry. *This is just an opportunity to see what God can do!*"

Mrs. H., in telling the story, said, "I was not going to let the little servant be better than I, so I got up and went about my work, but in my heart I kept saying, 'I will see what God can do.'

"About 11 o'clock, before we needed to put the potatoes on, a rap came at the door. On opening it, a man stood there and said, 'Are you Mrs. H.?'

" 'Yes,' I replied.

"The man told me he had come on the boat from Finland, where he had heard Mr. H. speak on China. He said, 'As I was coming to Stockholm, I thought I would bring a few bags of potatoes, as you might need them. And I just put along with them the half of a sheep!' " Mrs. H. ended the story by saying, "That is the way the Lord deals with me."

Chapter XIV

THE HOLY OF HOLIES

Christ in you, the hope of glory.
—Col. 1:27

Our 1916-17 FURLOUGH was an enforced one, owing to my husband's serious break in health.[1] On ariving in Toronto, we found the Missionary Rest Home a welcome refuge. Ruth was with us, and Paul soon joined us, a semi-invalid from the Great War. Helen, taking her nurse's course in the Toronto General Hospital, spent most of her off time with us. Our own room, a small one, became the rendezvous for us all.

It was while living under these circumstances that I received an urgent request for a brief story of God's dealing with me in a spiritual experience I had just passed through. I shrank from writing of such a sacred experience, but finally consented, only on condition that the Lord make it unmistakably plain it was according to His will. To attempt to write such a story without time for quiet waiting on the Lord—I could not.

---

[1] *Goforth of China*, chap. XVII.

So, without saying a word to anyone, even my husband, I asked the Lord for a sign—it was to give me our room, all to myself, for one week! I just left the matter in this way and waited.

Two days later a friend called. Before she left, it was arranged that all of us would accompany her to Muskoka for the summer. We were to be ready to start two days later. I thought, "This means I am not to write that story." Then Helen arrived, and, on hearing our plans for Muskoka, exclaimed, "But, Mother, *you* are not to go with the others. I'm to have my tonsils out, and I want you to visit me each day of the week I am to be in bed!" As I listened to my daughter, I could only sit quite still in wonder and awe at the way the Lord had wrought for me. Of that God-given, quiet, restful week, alone with God, I cannot write except to say the story was written as He guided.

The experience I am about to record covers, in part, the testimony referred to. It was written and published over twenty years ago but is such a vital part of my life's story that it cannot be withheld from these pages.

On our first arrival home, many requests came for my husband to take meetings. When it became known that he could not, I was urged to take his place. But the months of ceaseless overland travel through inland China with my husband, who was evidently breaking, the nursing, and the anxiety had all told on me. I felt physically worn, spiritually dead, and mentally numb. But deep in my heart I craved for some fresh spiritual blessing, for fresh vision that might enable me to speak once more out of an overflowing heart.

How true, how very true is the sentiment expressed in the following lines:

> Thy soul must overflow
> If thou another soul woulds't reach;
> It needs the overflow of heart
> To give the lips full speech!

The tender, loving Lord saw just what His child needed and once again worked for her beyond all she could ask or think.

We had been but a short time at the rest home when a friend carried me off, insisting that I needed a rest. She took me to Niagara-on-the-Lake, where a Bible conference was being held. There I found myself in a beautiful hotel room with my friends nearby. The following morning we gathered under some trees by the auditorium before the meeting. The scenery was wonderful to me after poor, dried-up China. Through the trees could be glimpsed the beautiful Niagara river flowing down till it entered the lake. Begging my friends to leave me there, I gave myself to the exquisite enjoyment of my surroundings.

A short time passed. Suddenly there came an impelling to enter the auditorium. I obeyed, but, the place being full, I walked forward and finally found a seat immediately in front of the pulpit. The speaker was just beginning his address. He was a stranger, but from almost his first sentence his message gripped me.

He drew simply but vividly, first a picture of an ordinary, all too common Christian life. If he had drawn the picture from my everyday life experience, he could not have given it other than he did—sometimes on the mountaintop with visions of God and His mighty power; then the sagging, the dimming of vision, coldness, discouragement, even definite disobedience and a time of downgrade experience. Again through some sorrow or trial, there would come a return and seeking of the Lord, with again the higher Christian experiences. In a word, the speaker pictured an up-and-down life of intermingled victory and defeat.

The speaker then asked all who truly sought for God's highest and best, yet who knew the picture he had drawn was true of their Christian life and experience, to hold up their hands. Being in the front seat and realizing many behind knew who I was, and that they thought of me as a "good missionary," I kept my hand down. It was too humiliating to acknowledge *that* picture as representing me! But the Spirit of God strove with me. "If you keep your hand down you are a hypocrite! If you truly want God's best, humble yourself." So up went my hand.

Then the speaker drew another picture: it was the Christian life as God had not only *planned* it for His children but had made abundant provision for their living it. He described it as a life of victory, not defeat, of peace and trust, not struggle and worry. All through his address, I kept thinking, "Yes, it's wonderful, but I've tried so often and failed; I doubt if it is possible." Then the speaker ended by urging us to go over the texts listed on a slip of paper to be given free at the close of the meeting. He emphasized the importance of standing on God's Word.

The following morning I rose early, as soon as it was light enough to see. On my knees, I read from the list I have mentioned all the texts given. But before I had gone halfway down the list, I saw clearly that God's Word taught, beyond the shadow of a doubt, that *the overcoming, victorious life in Christ is the normal life God has planned for His children*. In the two days that followed clearer light came, with a dawning hope that this life might be possible for me.

When returning home by boat to Toronto, an American tourist from the southern states and I discussed what we had been hearing at the conference. Our experiences were very similar. On parting, we gave each other our addresses, with the compact that if he found the secret of the victorious life he would write to me and if I found it I would write to him. (Unfortunately I lost his address.)

The day after reaching home, I picked up the little booklet, *The Life That Wins*, and, going to my son's bedside, I asked him to allow me to read the booklet aloud, as it was the personal testimony of Charles G. Trumbull, editor of the *Sunday School Times*, the man who had been a great blessing to me at the conference.

As I began to read, quite a number gathered around, listening with deep interest. I read on till I came to the words: "At last I realized that Jesus Christ was actually and literally within me." I stopped amazed. The sun seemed suddenly to come from under a cloud and flood my soul with light! How blind I had been! I saw as in a flash the secret of victory. *It was just Jesus Christ Himself!*

But the thought of victory was for the moment lost sight of in the inexpressible joy of the new vision and realization of Christ.

For days I seemed as if in a dream. Fearing lest I be, as it were, "carried off my feet," by what had come to me, I determined to seek the advice of one who had for many years been our beloved and honored foreign missionary secretary, the Rev. Dr. R. P. McKay, a man known for his sanctity and common sense. (My husband was away, as I remember.)

Never can I forget a detail of that interview. Dr. McKay listened sympathetically while I told all. I ended by saying, "Do you think I am going too far in this? I have just sent off to missionaries in China fifty copies of the booklet, *The Life that Wins.*"

Dr. McKay smiled as he replied, "No, Mrs. Goforth, for I have just sent out to ministers and others several hundred copies of the same booklet."

Then he gravely added: "Mrs. Goforth, I am amazed—amazed that you have only now come to apprehend this truth of Christ's indwelling. You have been the wife of Jonathan Goforth for many years. His messages were aglow with this truth. IT IS THE HOLY OF HOLIES OF OUR CHRISTIAN FAITH."

"Yes, Dr. McKay," I replied humbly, "I begin to realize this and wonder at my blindness. One sentence my husband so often uses has come back to me these days: All the resources of the Godhead are at our disposal!"

Dr. McKay then said: "It seems that this, the deepest truth, the union of the divine and human, is not received by simple head knowledge but must be apprehended through the Holy Spirit's revealing."

I left Dr. McKay strengthened in the belief that what had come to me was indeed of the Holy Spirit. But I was determined to search the Scriptures and stand only on them. That summer I laid aside all secular reading and, with a concordance, dug into my Bible, and, oh, the wonderful treasures I found! The line of study was entirely on the union of the divine and human.[2]

Later I discovered that the words, "God would make known what is the riches of the glory of this mystery among the Gentiles; which is Christ in you, the hope of glory" (Col. 1:27), had changed the lives of many who later became marvelously used of God. The Rev. Dr. A. B. Simpson was but one of these.

Oh, beloved fellow-climbers, let us ask ourselves, "WHAT WOULD HAPPEN IF WE ALL BELIEVED GOD? Would we justify ourselves in speaking the irritable and irritating word? Would we dare spend time in reading that which would soil or desecrate the temple of Christ's pure Holy Spirit?" More than twenty years have gone by since I passed through the experience of which I have just written. Many, many times in these years have I been humbled and brought low be-

---

[2] *How I Know God Answers Prayer.*

cause of disobedience to the heavenly vision, but, praise God, His fountain of cleansing always has been open, and His heart of love always ready to forgive and renew. Indeed, as I look back over these past twenty years, the goodness of the Lord to me has been so great, His sustaining, protecting, guiding presence so manifest, I seem to lose sight of my failures in the multitude of His mercies. Truly, "He hath not dealt with us after our sins; nor rewarded us according to our iniquities" (Ps. 103:10).

The following story has been such a blessing to me that I want to pass it on to other climbers.

In a certain small town lived a blacksmith, a bad man, leader of the wildest set. This man became soundly converted, out and out for his new Master. One day, some months after the great change came, an old "pal" appeared at the forge.

"Look here," he said, "why don't you give up this whole religion business and come back to us? Ye have had a sight of trouble these months —sickness and death and what not, the like ye never had."

The blacksmith was working on an important spring. He motioned to the other to watch while he worked, silently heating pieces of metal red-hot, then joining to the spring. But at last a piece would not join, though he heated it again and again. It would not take the "temper" and had to be thrown on the scrap heap. Then, turning to his old comrade, the blacksmith said: "Since I gave myself to the Lord Jesus, I see *that's* the way He deals with His children. So I sez, 'O

Lord, hammer me all ye will, but don't throw me on the scrap heap!'"

Years have passed since hearing this story of the blacksmith; and many times when passing through some furnace experience have I, too, raised the cry, "Lord, hammer me all you will, but don't throw me on the scrap heap."

How often, throughout my long, changeful life, have I wondered at the Lord's patience with me! I know now why He never *threw me on the scrap heap*. He knew that when I confessed Him in the little Cross Sunday school room and took Him publicly as my Master, I was as sincere and wholly yielded as a child could be. He knew I based my acceptance on His own words, "Him that cometh to me I will in no wise cast out," and He kept His word.

We were still at the Missionary Rest Home in the summer of 1916 when I met with the following blessed experience, which taught the important lesson of being always a *ready* channel for God to use.

One morning, when ready to start for a day's shopping in the city (Toronto), I asked the Lord to enable me to bring a blessing to someone that day. To my disappointment, though I watched closely all day, no opening come. About sundown I reached the car terminal to see the Mimico car just disappearing. There would be a wait of twenty-five or thirty minutes, so I returned to the waiting room and seated myself on a long bench not far from a woman intent on reading a newspaper, which, to my surprise, proved to be the *Sunday School Times!* A thrill of joy came with the realization that this was my opportunity. So, sidling up to the woman, I said, "What a wonderful paper that is!"

For a moment the woman looked resentful, but softened and replied, "Yes, but there is so much I can't understand. How I wish I had someone to explain about this victorious life of which Mr. Trumbull writes so much."

Struggling with the deep emotion I was feeling, I told her of my prayer that morning, of what Mr. Trumbull had meant to me at the Niagara Conference, and how God had used him to open my blind eyes to the glorious teaching of Christ's indwelling through the Holy Spirit. The woman grasped my hand in both of hers and listened hungrily as I was speaking. All too soon the Mimico car was heard.

As we parted, the woman said, "Surely God led you to me. You have given me just what I needed."

Though we knew each other but a few brief moments, we parted like old friends, bound by the marvelous tie of Christian love. Oh, the inexpressible joy of such an evidence of Christ's own presence!

One of the great regrets now as I look back on life, is that I so seldom gave the Lord a chance to use me—so often too busy—too much taken up by lesser things to heed the cry of souls at hand!

In closing this most sacred, intimate chapter of these memories, the question faces me, Should I withhold an incident which tells of progress—of victory? I have been frank in revealing struggles and failures. Surely it will encourage you, my fellow-climbers, to tell also of what the apprehension of the Lord Jesus Christ meant in after life.

On our journey back to China after that 1916-17 furlough, I often talked with my dear husband of the future, wondering if the Lord would ever give me the joy of knowing I had in some measure retrieved that which I knew had followed me down through the years: *"If she would only live more as she preaches."* Oh, how I longed to live so that the Chinese could see Christ in me. My impatience and quickness of speech were my besetting sins. Many a man had I trained to be an efficient cook and really valuable servant only to lose him suddenly because of my lack of patience, giving a rebuke well deserved perhaps, but given in anger.

Many months (I forget just how long) had passed after our return to our Changte station when one evening one of our leading evangelists came in just when my husband was about to start for the street chapel. The evangelist showed plainly he wished to speak to my husband alone, so I left the room. When he had gone, I returned to find my husband standing by the table with a strange look on his face. He seemed deeply moved, yet glad. I exclaimed, "Whatever is the matter?"

"Rose," he said, "you could never guess what he came for. He came as a deputation from the other evangelists and workers, yes, and servants, too, to ask what is the secret of the change in you. Before you went home, none of the servants wanted to serve you, but now they all want to be your servants."

Is it any wonder tears flowed for very joy? But as if to test to the utmost, the Lord was even then preparing a furnace "seven times heated" through which, in the days soon to come, we were to pass.

Later that wonderful passage in the book of Joel came to have a new and blessed meaning to me:

I will restore to you the years that the locust hath eaten.—Joel 2:25

CHAPTER XV

MANCHURIAN MERCIES

Go . . . and tell . . . how great things the Lord hath done for thee.[1]—*Our Lord Jesus*

From the time of my conversion, when a young girl, the above words have come to me again and again as a direct command from the Master Himself. Nothing so inspired and strengthened faith in those early, impressionable years as hearing a clear, ringing testimony to God's power or grace or to some definite answer to prayer.

So, dear fellow-climbers, I desire that these final pages may be just a "call back" message, telling of the Lord's faithfulness to keep through storm and tempest, "even to hoar hairs." [2]

When, after church union, the field in which we had been laboring became the province of the United Church and my husband was asked by our Presbyterian Board to undertake the important mission of securing a new field in China,

[1] Mark 5:19.
[2] Isa. 46:4.

it seemed quite out of the question that I could possibly accompany him. I was very ill, but as he stood by my couch with the cable calling for his immediate return to China in his hand, he said, "I ought to go, but I dare not leave you as you are."

For only a brief moment I closed my eyes and prayed, "Lord, show me what I should do."

Then, clearly came the answer, "Go with him."

Looking up, I said: "Jonathan, I'm going with you." And even as I spoke, the thought came, "I would rather die with him, when traveling, than die alone here."

It was a step of faith, and by taking it I learned how marvelously the Lord could work for me—so much so I was even encouraged to ask for strength to deliver a brief message at our farewell meeting in Knox Church, Toronto, a few days later. This I did only by His enabling.

How can I tell in one brief paragraph the story of the following nine months? I traveled almost constantly, while day by day going down ever deeper into the valley of the shadow until, at last, on a stretcher, I entered the great Rockefeller Foundation Hospital at Peking.

One month later the doctors were rejoicing over the fact that the rigid diet prescribed by them had been demonstrated a success, for had I not actually gained several ounces in the course of the month? (A loss of over fifty pounds had been registered in the previous eighteen months.) So once again He brought me through!

But the hard two years' fight back to health

had only begun when the call to Manchuria came.

Before passing from that year of supreme testing, I would like to give a "call back" testimony to the Lord's keeping power in the hour of weakness and suffering. All through those months He revealed Himself in a most blessed way, giving rest and peace of spirit I had never known before.

On reaching Manchuria, which has a climate as cold as central Canada in the most bitter midwinter zero weather, we had three months of waiting at a strange station before a way opened to make our mission headquarters at Szepingkai. To save the time of others, for our band was small, I simply gave myself to obeying the strict injunctions necessary to win the battle back to health. It seemed a selfish life. Often I became discouraged and wondered how I could bear to live on the foreign field without some definite ministry of my own.

Then the time came when we moved to Szepingkai to the upper room over the chapel and Chinese quarters, which was to be our mission home. Too weak to ascend or descend the ladder-like steps leading to the court below, the future looked black for me.

Then (oh, praise the Lord!) He opened to me a ministry that later was declared by all to be second to none in importance!

Our little band had settled in Szepingkai but a short time when my husband was led to take the step of faith for Chinese evangelists and money for their support. This story has been told

more fully in *Goforth of China*. The Lord so
honored this step of faith that before many weeks
passed it became evident to all that someone
must give much time to the secretary-treasurer-
ship of the evangelistic funds now coming in ever
increasing volume for the support of evangelists.
(Before many months the number of evangelists
had increased from six to sixty.) As the number
increased, in like proportion, gifts came for their
support, absolutely unsolicited, chiefly from the
United States.

All of our small band of only five missionaries
except myself were almost overwhelmed with the
responsibilities of the work. So it came about that
the secretarial work was laid on me. From the
first, I felt it to be a God-given ministry. The increasingly great correspondence it entailed,
though at times almost too strenuous, was a
great joy. My co-workers assured me it was as
vital a part as any in the evangelization of our
vast, needy field.

Most of the donations were quite small. Some
were touching. I may take space to mention but
two of the many hundreds of letters and donations received.

A postal order for three shillings from London, England came accompanied only by a torn
slip of paper on which was written in a shaking
hand: "From an old woman on an old age pen-
sion, to help make Jesus known."

The other I shall mention was from a little boy
in Winnipeg. His mother wrote that one morning the boy came and emptied his moneybox in
her lap, saying, "Mother, I dreamed last night

I was fighting with those terrible heathen bandits in Manchuria. I want you to send this to Dr. Goforth to help tell about Jesus." He then ran off to school. A moment later he appeared, saying: "Mother, don't delay, but send the money off at once. *I don't want the Lord to tell me to do it the second time.*"

Some time later, I told this story to an audience in Boston. At the close of my address, the chairman rose and said: "Although we have taken up a collection, I'm going to give all who feel like that boy—that you don't want the Lord to tell you the second time—another opportunity to give." The collection taken, and later given to us, was sufficient to support at least two evangelists in Manchuria for a year.

As I attempt to recall those years in Manchuria, there comes to mind the numerous occasions when the Lord undertook for us in cases of illness. Having no doctor or nurse in our mission, we could only look to our never-failing Lord when sudden acute illness came.

One outstanding experience I shall endeavor to give somewhat fully, as it lifts the veil on conditions as we faced them at that time.

The city of Taonan, a most important center bordering on Mongolia, was reached from Szepingkai in about nine hours by express train. Our young colleague, the Rev. Allan Reoch, had been left in charge of the work there during the summer of 1938. But it was thought best my husband should be with him for at least a few months to lay the foundations of such an important center. On our return from a long mission journey to Indochina, we moved from Szepingkai to Taonan.

Most alarming reports were rife of bubonic plague spreading rapidly along the railway westward toward Taonan. A few days after our arrival there, the report came of twenty-five deaths from plague having taken place in one small section of the city. Then the Japanese took charge of plague suppression and as a result, no doubt, multitudes of lives were saved, for the plague was stayed.

It is quite a personal story that now follows. Perhaps some will say that it is too personal! I give it for the first and only time, believing it will be to the "glory of His grace."

The only room available for us in the Chinese mission home in Taonan was at the end of a row of rooms. It was in an isolated part of the courtyard. Heavy rains had fallen during the summer. On the roof immediately over the corner of our room an eaves trough had been emptying volumes of water all summer into a hole in the ground just below. Unknown to anyone the water had been seeping down under and into the earthen floor of our room. When we entered the room, the floor was so wet we were obliged to put on rubbers and, when sitting, to keep our feet on bricks. The mud wall close beside my bed was so damp and soft I could press my fingers, without effort, inches into the wall. My husband loosened the many-ply wall paper some three feet above the floor and, to our horror, found literally thousands of small gray "dampbugs" scurrying for cover.

It may not surprise anyone to hear the result. Within a week tonsillitis had laid me low. Then when still weak, but with temperature normal, I again faced the *conditions*. After only a day or two lumbago and sciatica laid me low again. Two pretty hard weeks followed. Then inflammatory rheumatism of the joints started. By this time I had begun to realize that the conditions under which we were living were impossible, at least for me. My husband seemed in no way affected. He was, however, greatly troubled about me. But what could he do? We had come to give the winter to the Taonan field.

Then, as often before, we were to see what God could do.

Realizing that I needed to get to a dry, sunny place, I cried to the Lord with the cry of desperation to open a way to return to Szepingkai, for, though the place there was somewhat barnlike, it was high and dry and sunny.

A day or two later a letter came from the evangelists at Szepingkai, urging my husband's immediate return, as there was no one to take charge of the work there. After consultation with Mr. Reoch, it was decided that we should leave for Szepingkai at once. I could see God's hand working.

But the most wonderful evidence of His divine power was yet to come. Reaching Szepingkai, I kept going the first day or two. Then what seemed like all the pent-up virus of rheumatism centered in my hip. I became very ill with high fever and agonizing pain. A day passed. Then suddenly my heart seemed to be giving out. It would jolt and stop for so long that I would open my eyes, wondering that I was still alive. My husband was at his desk.

"Jonathan," I whispered, "feel my pulse."

Immediately he felt the pulse and said: "Don't stir; I'll pray." His face was white, but as he prayed, my pulse began to steady. In a short time it seemed quite normal. The fever and pain had lessened. Two days later I was around as usual, with a song of joy and gratitude in my heart.

Why are we so prone to deny to the Lord credit for what is distinctly evident as the result of *His* working?

The following is, to me, one of the most blessed experiences in my whole life of God's understanding and interest in me.

From the time we moved to Szepingkai in April, 1927, until the autumn of 1933, our only bedroom was a screened-off portion of a large room over the chapel. The rest of the room was used as study and sitting room. It was the general rendezvous for all missionaries, where prayer meetings and important interviews with Chinese leaders were held. Indeed it was in winter the only safe place to keep perishable things, as vegetables, fruits, etc. from freezing (carefully packed under the bed!), as we had no storeroom.

The Chinese are gifted with at least an ordinary (some say extraordinary) amount of curiosity and have a very dexterous and satisfying way of attaining vantage for sight through paper windows and screens. It is simple and silent. The middle finger of the right hand is moistened with saliva, then applied gently to the paper with a circular, rubbing movement which soon results in a tiny hole large enough for the pupil of the eye to take in what is on the other side of the paper screen. I found that even a Japanese screen is not entirely impervious to this plan.

Such conditions were not "ideal." Sometimes, I fear, I was hard to get along with, especially during the first year when I was fighting desperately but successfully to regain strength after the attack of sprue. I do not want to justify myself, however, for I know God's grace would have been sufficient to keep me calm and sweet *always,* but sometimes I just failed my Master. On the whole, those years were busy, happy years, though at times extremely testing.

Then, in April of 1933, my beloved husband became blind. One result was that Chinese evangelists and leaders were constantly coming to see him. Very often, for many hours together, the "sitting" part of our room was filled. I literally had no place for quiet when working at my desk, as I had to, many hours a day, nor, indeed, for a moment of assured privacy.

I began to get nervous. More and more the need for a bedroom to myself became an urgent necessity. Yet there seemed no possible way to get one. Oh, how I prayed, but no light came.

Then one night, when at an outstation with my husband, I could not sleep. I kept praying to the Lord to open up some way for me to get a quiet *private* room. Suddenly, in the dark I saw before me a plan, clear and distinct, as if it were sketched on paper. To my amazement, this plan revealed that by taking down a wooden partition, changing one door and adding another, our room next to our sitting room could be made into a fair-sized bedroom and the adjoining hall into a bathroom.

The following morning, when I told my husband he was delighted. After a little thought, he said, "I think you can even have a storeroom by using part of the hall for that purpose!" No time was lost on our returning to Szepingkai in carrying out the plan. In less than a month, we were settled in our comfortable suite consisting of sitting room, bedroom, bathroom, and storeroom —at a cost of less than twelve dollars. Ingenuity was needed to find places here and there for trunks, etc. A place was found in the lower court for stoves, pipes, and such articles.

But, oh, the blessedness of at last having a room where one could lock the door and be alone! I know God gave the vision. Praise His name!

For just one year we were permitted to enjoy the luxury of that extra room. We thanked God many times for what we both felt to be our God-given refuge. Especially was this so during my husband's serious illness and later at the time of my collapse, when we were both hurried back to Canada.

What can I write now other than has been written of eighteen strenuous months together holding meetings through eastern Canada till the morning when I awoke to find my companion, friend, husband, and hero of almost fifty years had passed through the invisible but impenetrable Veil quietly, in his sleep.

Then followed the greatest miracle of my life —the writing of his wonderful life, *Goforth of China.*

The time has come when visions of the past must fade as we turn toward the summit now almost in sight—so near a trace may be seen of the glory awaiting us when we reach the end of the road. Not the foot of the hill, as some have said, for that would lead us back into the Valley of Shadows, but rather to the summit, from whence may be glimpsed the glorious light of the Celestial City.

As we think of these things, one more vision of the far past comes:

Once again I seem to be a little child facing my desk in the old schoolroom. The evening shadows have lengthened, and the ending of the day's work has come. The rustle of putting away books and pencils has ceased. All sit upright, quietly watching the master's hand poised above the bell ready to give the signal for the pupils to rise and return home.

So once again at the close of life's little day, the pen must be laid aside as we await in quietness and in confidence the signal from the Master's hand to rise and GO HOME.

Epilogue

God did great things for the Goforths in Manchuria 1927-1935

I. *God Sustained them even in sickness and in old age.*

Nearing 70, Jonathan Goforth refused to go home to Canada and "sit in a rocking chair and wait to die." He was even undaunted by the civil war raging throughout China where he had given a lifetime to preaching the Gospel. Word reached him of a vacant mission field in Manchuria of 3 million people and he immediately accepted it. Rosalind demonstrated unbelievable courage and fortitude by insisting on accompanying Jonathan, though she was suffering from the deadly disease of sprue— a chronic dysentery.

For eight years the Goforths worked to establish churches over a vast area in Manchuria paying little heed to the appalling hardships.

II. *God Protected them even from Bandits and Plague.*

This quote will give a flash of light on the conditions at that time: "Just north of Szepingkai, our main station, 30 women were carried off by bandits and a great feast was made and all 30 women were forced to go through the marriage ceremony which binds them as wives to these men. Sometimes our hearts sicken at the apparent hopelessness of the state of things in China. We just go on and reach as many as we can with the Gospel."

Mother tells of the awful bubonic plague raging all around them, while they are on a country preaching tour. Typically she remarks in brackets ("no one ever recovers from this kind of plague.")

I can't imagine how they endured the dead of winter in Manchuria—biting winds off the bleak Mongolian deserts—inadequate house heat, revealed in this remark: "The basin of water at our bedside is often solid ice in the morning."

III. *God supplied their needs.*

A few missionaries rallied around the Goforths. But the great need was for trained native workers. Father in a great explosion of faith and zeal appealed to the Canadian Presbyterian Mission Board for "50 young men to evangelize this great field God has given us." The answer was "we can't send you one!" It was the time of the Great Depression.

Father was driven to his knees and he begged God to send the men and the money. And, that is exactly what He did! Dr. John Hayes of a Shantung seminary wrote Father "I have a class of 60 grads I cannot place because of chaotic conditions in China. Can you use any of them?" Father's reply was, "Send them all!" Mother, the practical one, said "How on earth are we going to feed all those men and their families?" But God sent the money in unsolicited gifts from all over the world. Thus a great work of *FAITH* began!

IV. *God gave Fruit for their Labors.*

One exciting report from Father was: "Mary, I am having an average of 10 conversions a day! What a harvest!"

Opening a new work at Taonanfu was very strenuous. This incident reveals the character of Jonathan Goforth, the pioneer. "Father was sitting in an old, broken easy chair in front of the stove. A look of absolute happiness (at 70!) came over his face as he said, 'Oh, is it not grand to be out here to open up such a place to the Gospel! Why, I'd rather be just here than in Windsor Castle!' "

48 congregations were organized in those eight years—the churches being built by the people themselves—who also undertook the support of their pastors. This became in deed and in fact a truly indigenous work.

After my parents died, the Japanese-Chinese war continued for 14 years. At the end of that time missionaries who were able to return to the field of the Canadian Presbyterian Mission found 47 of those 48 churches still carrying on!

When I visited Manchuria in 1980 I found a work being done by the daughter of Father's most valued preacher companion Pastor Su. Her name is Su sai-guang and she is a preacher at Changchun. Her letters are a great inspiration. There were terrible massacres of Christians in the Changchun area. She reports: "We started a few years ago in a small room. Now we have 600 believers attending. Just recently 120 were baptized and there are more to come." I can almost hear the rejoicing up there in Heaven!

V. *God rewarded their sacrificial giving.*

This facet of my parents lives has left an indelible imprint on my life. I can still hear Father declaiming "You cannot outgive God!" "Sow sparingly and you will reap sparingly!" "Go all out for God and He will go all out for you!" How wonderfully they exemplified that great verse in II Chron. 16:9 (Liv. Bible). Their hearts were "perfect toward God" so He literally "used His great power in helping them!"

After Mother died, my husband Bob Moynan went to the Bank of Commerce on Yonge Street in downtown Toronto to close out the account for the Goforth Evangelistic Fund. The manager said in amazement: "More money has passed through this Goforth Account than any other in this bank!" We knew the secret was because God kept His promise and had opened the windows of heaven. Three million dollars was offered by a lady in the United States just before Father died. He took this as a beautiful seal of God's favor on his conviction that in all mission work evangelism should be the main thrust.

VI. *God helped them make a Permanent Record to His Glory.*

"By My Spirit" by Jonathan Goforth, has had an almost uprecedented run of over 50 years. It is the story of his revival ministry throughout China. It has long been "must" reading in seminaries and Bible schools. I give here just one of thousands of testimonies. Rev. Dwight Kinman of Tacoma—a hospital chaplain and one of the godliest men I know says, "That book, given to me by my mother as a young man, has moulded my life."

Rosalind Goforth wrote six books to God's great glory. "Goforth of China"—"Climbing"—"How I Know God Answers Prayer"—are listed as "all time missionary classics." Now, "Climbing" her autobiography is being reprinted, including some pictures. May this generation be greatly blessed by it—just as their parents have been.

by Mary Goforth Moynan